MW00986134

MANAGEMENT
BY
PROVERBS

MANAGEMENT BY PROVERBS

APPLYING TIMELESS WISDOM IN THE WORKPLACE

MICHAEL A. ZIGARELLI, PH.D.

MOODY PRESS
CHICAGO

For Tara,
my wife, my friend, and my editor.

You bring meaning to the words:
"A wife of noble character
who can find?
She is worth far more than rubies.
Her husband has full
confidence in her
and lacks nothing of value.
She brings him good, not harm,
all the days of her life."
(Proverbs 31:10–12)

CONTENTS

ACKNOWLEDGMENTS

I am indebted to the assiduous folks at Moody Press who have offered their time and expertise to this project. Special thanks to Jim Vincent for his editorial fine-tuning and many insightful suggestions. My thanks also to Jim Bell and Bill Soderberg for their helpful guidance in tailoring the content to benefit a broad range of managers, from CEOs to first-time supervisors, from pastors to those managing charities. They have greatly enhanced the quality of this book.

INTRODUCTION

WHY MANAGE
BY
PROVERBS?

The problems were at best tenacious, if not insurmountable. Robert Frey had recently purchased Cin-Made Corporation, a small company in Cincinnati that manufactured mailing tubes, composite cans, and sturdy paper containers. For a quarter of a century Cin-Made had been run by an autocratrix who worked eighty-hour weeks to micromanage every detail of the operation. As a result, almost all the unionized workforce of a few dozen employees viewed management as an adversary. Relations with the union were contentious, job definitions were narrow and rigid, and workers simply put in their eight-hour days, indifferent to company profits or losses.

To make matters worse, labor costs were out of control and continuing to spiral. A collective bargaining agreement granted employees a 27 percent pay hike over three years, and union members expected this wage trajectory would continue unabated. Any attempt to temper this trend would surely be met by a strike during the next round of negotiations.

Cin-Made's employee problems reverberated through its sales and distribution systems. More than a quarter of all shipments arrived late, and the company was on the verge of losing its top customer. Profits, which had hovered between 1 and 2 percent of sales for some time, had dropped to zero with the new labor contract, and the highly competitive market in which Cin-Made operated was intensifying.[1]

FINDING ANSWERS FROM THE PAST

What could Frey do to turn around his newly acquired company? Throughout the past two hundred years, management and economic theorists have postulated remedies to the condition that ailed Cin-Made. But employee-management theory is much older than that; we can in fact trace the theories to the days of Israel's first lawgiver, Moses.

Like the doyenne who previously owned Cin-Made, Moses took a faulty step, insisting on making every decision and adjudicating all of the disputes for his people. In Exodus 18 his father-in-law, Jethro, offered an astute observation: "What you are doing is not good. You and these people who come to you will only wear yourselves out" (17–18). As the first scripturally recorded management consultant, Jethro offered an additional insight: "Select capable men from all the people . . . and appoint them as officials over thousands, hundreds, fifties and tens" (21). Cin-Made's former owner, according to the Jethro school of thought, should have begun to address the problems by creating a bureaucracy of "capable" middle managers.

Fast-forward a few thousand years and we see men like Adam Smith, John Stuart Mill, and David Ricardo advancing a neoclassical economic perspective on employee management: Treat labor and capital as substitutes for one another. This paradigm manifested itself, during America's Industrial Revolution, as the "drive system," and it represents another possible approach for Cin-Made: To motivate workers, constantly supervise them, use a lot of profanity, regularly threaten dismissal, and occasionally speed up production to remind them who's in charge. Could this be the elixir for Cin-Made's ills?

Some would argue instead that Cin-Made needs to adopt "scientific management," a somewhat less barbaric approach from Frederick Taylor. Using engineering principles, Taylor conducted time-motion studies and determined how many seconds each human task should require and what it was worth. He advocated compensating people based exclusively on what they produced. Perhaps piecework is the answer for Robert Frey.

Another option for Frey is to take a more paternalistic approach. This century, the notion dates back to two wealthy and innovative practitioners of capitalism: Henry Ford and John D. Rockefeller Jr. Ford's theory was to pay what we now call an "efficiency wage"—a well-above-market five dollars a day in 1914—to motivate employees to work harder, to obey company rules, to live a life of good character outside the workplace. The hypothesis of his contemporary, evangelical Christian CEO John Rockefeller Jr., was that one could best affect productivity and retention through "welfare capitalism," a system whereby employees would receive not only a decent wage, but a home, adequate rest, free medical and dental care, paid vacations, a pension, and input into managerial decision making.[2]

Finally, Frey could accept the current thinking on employee management, treating employees as an investment rather than a cost. With a nod toward Rockefeller's once-radical notions, "high performance work practices" are touted as a possible panacea to the timeless questions about employee productivity that plagued Mr. Frey and countless others who have served in a managerial capacity.[3] Ken Blanchard, author of *One Minute Manager* and many other best-selling business books, plainly noted that "You will get little argument today if you tell managers that people are their most important resource."[4] Similarly, Peter Drucker, often cited as the father of contemporary management theory, wrote: "Executives spend more time on managing people and making people decisions than on anything else—and they should."[5]

Indeed, companies have historically expended much energy developing and testing philosophies of employee management. But owing to the unpredictable, often uncontrollable human variables in the system, we have yet to construct an ideal cause-and-effect model that both optimizes organizational performance and generalizes across time and environments.

So we cannot give Frey a simple, absolute answer. And further complicating any theory of employee management are the ethical concerns.

Managing people—men and women with personal aspirations, familial obligations, and souls—presents us with unique and irritating issues when developing a managerial formula.

I should explicitly note at the outset that the content of this book makes no claim on that elusive, all-encompassing formula. This project can simply be regarded as part of the distinguished tradition of theorizing about employee management.

However, what this book does claim is that the "theory" herein is of a different genre, since it is borne not out of empirical observation and human inference, but out of a book from the sacred canon. The nineteen managerial principles found in this text are grounded entirely in the wisdom of the Book of Proverbs.

A PROFILE OF THE BOOK OF PROVERBS

Renowned Bible teacher Chuck Swindoll characterizes the Book of Proverbs as "the most practical book in the Old Testament and, in many ways, the most practical book in all the Bible."[6] A counterpart to Psalms, which furnishes insight into how to relate to God, Proverbs offers counsel on how people should relate to one another and to the world around them. The book contains wise counsel in making business decisions and understanding people, including those we work with Monday through Friday.

Before we glean the management principles from this God-inspired resource, a little background about the book. Structurally, Proverbs spans thirty-one chapters and primarily contains the sayings of Solomon, Israel's third and wisest king (1 Kings 3:12). The book also includes the "Sayings of the Wise," and of Agur (Proverbs 22:17–24:34 and Proverbs 30, respectively). It concludes with the "Sayings of King Lemuel" and the epilogue about the wife of noble character (Proverbs 31). The majority of its contents are traditionally dated to the tenth century B.C.

In contrast to the history, biography, and prophecy of the rest of the Old Testament, Proverbs is a philosophical book that seeks to answer the eternal question: "How should we live?" As such, it speaks to every life issue of consequence, and, not surprisingly, it affords us an impressive amount of guidance in business matters. Borrowing from the work of Roy B. Zuck, Table 1 summarizes those themes with the most patent application to management.[7]

Table 1

PROVERBS THEMES APPLICABLE
TO MANAGEMENT

PROVERBS THEME	SPECIFIC GUIDANCE
Advice to leaders	Be honest, humble, just, reliable, self-controlled and sober.
Money	Avoid get-rich-quick schemes, unfair pricing, charging exorbitant interest rates, and bribery; recognize consequences of gaining money dishonestly, money's ability to motivate people to work; share money liberally with the poor.

Proverbs Theme	Specific Guidance
Proper use of words	Use words to impart wisdom, encourage, protect, and nurture.
Improper use of words	Avoid lying, slander, gossip, false witnessing, mocking, perverse talk, boasting, flattery, or quarreling.
Virtues	Show courage, diligence, humility, generosity, honesty, integrity, kindness (to poor, to needy, to animals), love, patience, self-control, reliability, sobriety, teachability, and truthfulness.
Vices	Don't acquire money dishonestly, be angry or lose temper, bribe, be drunken, envious, greedy, hypocritical, unjust, jealous, lazy, oppress the poor, or be proud.
Work and family	Be faithful to spouse; show priority of spouse and children over work.

When we apply Proverbs' principles for human relationships to the workplace, they offer guidance for (1) building a competitive workforce, (2) cultivating a culture of commitment, (3) evaluating and rewarding performance, and (4) minimizing strife. We will explore each of these four areas in parts 2 through 5. First, however, we should consider Proverbs' contemporary relevance and review some rules for its responsible interpretation. We then will look at (in part 1) some personal attitudes and attributes of the manager who will be most effective in applying Proverbs' principles in the workplace. Why not just proceed to Proverbs' application to traditional business functions? you may ask. Because effective application of Proverbs' content depends on accurate interpretation and being able to recognize our personal attitudes. This is fundamental for achieving long-term success in management by proverbs. Ignore this foundation, and you may find yourself achieving few desired results and, ultimately, abandoning the effort completely.

WHY THE ANCIENT PROVERBS?

The threshold question that arises in any study of this nature is: "Why Proverbs?" Why use ideas from another time and culture? Are they truly superior to the ideas that are contemporary to our experience? To answer this, let's first look to the credentials of its authors.

Solomon and Business

As noted earlier, most of the proverbs are from the mind of King Solomon. The king achieved notoriety for many things: for building a magnificent temple, for keeping a politically divided nation intact, for having 700 wives and 300 concubines, and for writing 3,000 proverbs and 1,005 hymns. (See 1 Kings 11:3; 4:32.) Still, John Bright, perhaps the foremost Old Testament historian of our day, wrote that "Solomon's true genius . . . lay in the realm of industry and trade."[8]

Solomon knew business. Under his leadership, Israel's copper industry as well as its horse, chariot, and other trades were consolidated under a state-ownership umbrella and transformed into tremendously lucrative enterprises. Consequently, Israel accumulated vast riches and enjoyed unprecedented economic prosperity throughout this era. It is an astute businessman who offers us insights throughout Proverbs.

Still, Proverbs was written centuries ago. And it was composed by a CEO who was unencumbered by our present business realities and addressed to a culture vastly different from our own. Solomon did not live in a world of global competition, E-mail, and total quality management. He was accountable to no shareholders and did not have to bargain with any unions. He held monopoly power over every industry. He could rewrite any government policy he didn't like, and he could not be fired. Notwithstanding Solomon's managerial proficiency, the business environment of 900 B.C. was so incongruent with our own that applying his advice might not seem responsible, much less sagacious. Common sense would suggest, then, that the king's time- and culture-specific "wisdom" would not generalize across the millennia.

The Inspired Scriptures

Common sense, though, is often a blunt analytical tool for interpreting something as uncommon as Scripture. As we consider whether to apply three thousand year-old ideas, let's remember that the authors of Proverbs, like those in all the books recognized as Holy Scripture, are really co-authors with God. A central pillar of Christian theology is that the human authors of Scripture wrote under the inspiration of God's Holy Spirit (2 Timothy 3:16; 2 Peter 1:20–21). They were not taking dictation, nor were they required to compromise their personality or literary styles; but at the same time, they were not simply advancing their own personal theologies. The Spirit of God guided them to communicate a message intended not just for the writer's local community, but for all people across generations.

The Book of Proverbs, therefore, does not represent the ruminations of some pensive and perceptive king writing independently. These thoughts are not mere human musings about what worked in Solomon's personal and business affairs. They are, in fact, nothing less than God's counsel to His people, filtered through a messenger of His choosing.

And, despite the cultural differences three thousand years later, this divine advice informs us today with comparable force. This is because the central problem which Proverbs seeks to correct—a human nature that is bent on doing things its own way rather than God's way—is one that transcends generations, cultures, and circumstances. People remain prone to the greed, envy, dishonesty, and sharp tongues that typified those living in Solomon's day. It is still in our basic nature to set our own rules for relating to one another and to the world around us. This is what makes the Book of Proverbs so relevant to our lives thousands of years after Solomon's ink dried. Proverbs affords us insight into our shortcoming of self-reliance and all of its manifestations, and provides a road map to traverse the less-traveled paths of righteous behavior.

A proverb that succinctly and trenchantly warns against self-reliance and points to righteous behavior is one that many learned in Sunday school:

> *Trust in the Lord with all your heart*
> *and lean not on your own*
> *understanding; in all your ways*
> *acknowledge him, and he will*
> *make your paths straight.*
> (Proverbs 3:5–6)

Our perception of self-sufficiency, an obstinate leaning on our own understanding, is one of humanity's fatal flaws. It has been this way ever since the Garden of Eden. And it is for this very reason that Proverbs applies to each one of us today: It continues to represent God's unchanging counsel to His children, who are called to trust in Him.

INTERPRETING AND APPLYING THE PROVERBS

When it comes to properly interpreting and applying the Proverbs, we should recall Solomon's wise similes in Proverbs 26:7, 9:

> *Like a lame man's legs that hang*
> *limp is a proverb in the mouth of a fool. . . .*
> *Like a thornbush in a drunkard's*
> *hand is a proverb in the*
> *mouth of a fool.*

An inherent danger always exists when applying Scripture, especially short Scriptures like the proverbs. Without proper care, our misinterpretation of a proverb may render its wisdom, as taught by Proverbs 26:7, as powerless as a "lame man's legs."

For example, a person who misunderstands *fear* in Proverbs 1:7 ("The fear of the Lord is the beginning of knowledge") to mean "be afraid of God" rather than "be reverent of and deferential to God" (as revealed by the original Hebrew meaning), will likely have his relationship with God inhibited by terror of wrath and judgment. This person's intellectual and spiritual development will be stunted, as will his ability to think as God thinks and see as God sees, since his conception of God is one-dimensional. Sadly, the life-changing potential of this verse is relegated to lameness when its message is misconstrued.

Hasty interpretation of a proverb may have ramifications far beyond leaving its wisdom dormant: It may actually culminate in harm to oneself or others. This second cautionary note comes from Proverbs 26:9, which paints the unusual but vivid picture of a drunkard wielding a thornbush. Consider, for instance, the parent who reads into proverbial discipline no farther than "He who spares the rod hates his son" (Proverbs 13:24a). Bible-based disciplining of children is a relatively complex doctrine that surely cannot be reduced to a sound bite, much less half a proverb! When one attempts to do so, though, the potential for misunderstanding and subsequent damage is enormous. Not only is this person at risk of treating his children too harshly, but because he believes that he is acting on the authority of

Scripture, he may perpetuate this behavior regardless of its observed consequences.

The central instruction of these highlighted warnings is reasonably clear: One must vigilantly resist the superficial interpretation and application of Proverbs. Any reading of Scripture that neglects basic hermeneutical (interpretational) guidelines for extracting the Scriptures' wisdom may result in speculative, inaccurate, and even dangerous constructions of its meaning. In recognition of the admonitions in Proverbs 26 to handle the proverbs responsibly, I will use the following five safeguards to protect against cursory or inaccurate applications of Proverbs to employee management:

1. Interpret Proverbs by Tapping the Original Language

Like most of the Old Testament, Proverbs was initially written in Hebrew. And although the English translation certainly captures many of the book's insights, some important nuances of the Hebrew do not survive a translation process. Words that generally carry one connotation in English may have a different or additional contour in Hebrew that renders the English version a less than complete reflection of the original message. The "fool" in Proverbs 1:7, for example, is not just someone who is foolish. When we trace the word back to the Hebrew, *'eviyl (ev-eel')*, translated here as *fool*, is a person who is *morally deficient*. The word *'eviyl* comes from a root that means "to be perverse," and is used to describe those who are licentious, quarrelsome, and defiant when guilty.

Through tapping the original language, then, we gain additional and valuable information about the message of this proverb: When we turn our backs on God's wisdom, we are more than merely foolish. In fact, our morality has become suspect. So, when viewed through the Hebrew language lens, Proverbs 1:7 reveals a sharper diverging of the paths before us than would be implied by a flat reading of the translation. We can choose respect and reverence ("fear") and knowledge, or we can choose moral deficiency. There is no middle ground.

2. Interpret a Proverb in Light of Other Scriptures on the Topic

Principles of Scripture are multifaceted. Their total shape is typically manifest only when various passages that speak to the same theme are examined and assimilated. Conversely, if one impetuously analyzes and applies any verse in a vacuum, one runs the risk of severe misapplication.

"A bribe is a charm to the one who gives it; wherever he turns, he succeeds," declares Proverbs 17:8. Without further investigation of the biblical teaching on bribery, one might conclude based on this verse that bribery is not only sanctioned by Scripture, but it is advanced as a means to success! But that conclusion opposes the plain teaching of many other Scriptures, both in Proverbs and in other books of the Bible. (For example, see Exodus 23:8; Deuteronomy 27:25; Proverbs 6:35; 15:27; 29:4.) Since so many other passages speak of bribery as a transgression, Proverbs 17:8 should be interpreted consistently. In all likelihood, it represents a general observation about the perspective of those who offer bribes: They view them as an effective vehicle to get what they want. Without completing this topical study of bribery, the reader could easily rationalize a payoff on the basis of Proverbs 17:8.

Just as one piece of evidence does not indicate a trend, one proverb does not constitute a scriptural principle. Accordingly, to avoid such interpretational pitfalls, the highlighted proverbs in each chapter of this book are reinforced by other Scriptures on point.

3. Interpret Individual Proverbs in the Context of the Book's Central Theme

A basic rule of literary interpretation is that "a text without a context is a pretext." Typically, when interpreting a passage of the Bible, one must place the passage in logical context by examining (1) what comes before and after the passage, and (2) how the passage is related to the author's thesis. In doing so, the Bible student can minimize the specter of spurious or imprecise constructions.

For most proverbs, their adjacent verses are generally unrelated. That is, the immediate context of the proverb is limited to the proverb itself, not the neighboring text. As such, the "before and after" issue does not exist. That's simple enough. But still relevant—and some say central to the proper interpretation of Proverbs[9]—is understanding the proverb's relationship to the author's central message. The overarching theme of the Book of Proverbs is that two roads lie before us at all times. Moment to moment we have a choice to make regarding which road will wear our footprints. The high road is labeled "wisdom"—or sometimes "righteousness"; the low road, "folly"—or sometimes "wickedness." Chapters 1 through 9 of Proverbs are essentially an extended discourse on these paths, painting in broad strokes the nature and consequences of each. Table 2 (next page) summarizes the character of those two paths.

But so what? How is this topology important to interpreting the brief proverbs that follow in chapters 10 through 31?

Plain and simply, this topology is a critical interpretive filter that helps us understand the broader significance of a narrow teaching. Indeed, the two- and four-line proverbs that comprise the majority of the Book of Proverbs offer profound insights into relating to other people. But we should interpret them as more than this. These chapters fill in the particulars of the two paths that are abstractly depicted in chapters 1 through 9: the path of wisdom (or righteousness) and the path of folly (or wickedness).

For example, Proverbs 15:1 teaches us something about each path: "A gentle answer turns away wrath, but a harsh word stirs up anger." As we attempt to interpret its message, we should be sure to do so on two levels, one interpreting the word, the other applying it according to the theme. Gentleness should, on one level, be viewed as something that drains tensions; but in the bigger picture—the book's theme—gentleness typified in a gentle answer is a mark of one who pursues knowledge and who is devoted to the Lord. It is an attribute of those on wisdom's road. Harshness, by comparison, is on one level something that exacerbates conflict; more broadly, though, a harsh word is a sign that one is traveling the alternative path, the path of folly, wickedness, and moral deficiency. When we recognize and respect this second level of analysis, the compulsion to apply the instruction becomes stronger, perhaps even strong enough to direct one's behavior at the emotional moment when one is inclined to respond harshly.

We must not forget the impact of context. It is

Table 2

CHARACTERISTICS OF THE TWO PATHS
AS DESCRIBED IN PROVERBS 1 THROUGH 9

THE PATH OF WISDOM AND RIGHTEOUSNESS	THE PATH OF FOLLY AND WICKEDNESS
• Disciplined and prudent life (1:3)	• Exploit and harm the innocent (1:10–14; 6:17)
• Understand what is right, just, and fair (1:3; 2:9)	• Quick to sin (1:16; 6:18)
• Discretion (1:4; 2:11)	• Inevitable calamity (1:26–27)
• Safety (1:33; 3:23; 4:6)	• Distress and trouble (1:27)
• At ease with no fear of harm (1:33)	• Delight in wrongdoing (2:14)
• Knowledge of God (2:5)	• Deviousness (2:15)
• Avoidance of adultery (2:16)	• Wise in one's own eyes (3:7)
• Long life (3:1–2; 3:16)	• Withhold good from those who deserve it (3:27–28)
• Prosperity (3:2; 3:16; 8:18; 8:21)	• Plot harm (3:29; 6:14; 6:18)
• A good name (3:4)	• Falsely accuse (3:30; 6:19)
• Honor (3:35; 8:18)	• Seek to make people fall (4:16)
• Faithfulness to spouse (5:15–20)	• Oblivious to one's own folly (4:19)
• Strategic thinking (6:6–8)	• Perverse mouth and corrupt lips (4:24; 6:12)
	• Will ultimately relinquish one's wealth (5:10; 6:11)

THE PATH OF WISDOM AND RIGHTEOUSNESS	THE PATH OF FOLLY AND WICKEDNESS
• Hatred of evil, pride, arrogance, evil behavior, and perverse speech (8:13) • Blessedness (8:32; 8:34)	• Lazy (6:9–11) • Stir up dissension (6:14; 6:19) • Haughty eyes and a lying tongue (6:17) • Lusty (6:25) • Seducible (6:25–26; 7:21–23) • Sneaky (7:8–9) • Loud and defiant (7:11; 9:13) • Brazen (7:13) • On a highway to the grave (7:27) • Undisciplined (9:13) • Lacking in judgment (9:16)

easy to dismiss individual proverbs as trivial based on their seemingly narrow content. However, when we interpret this content in the context of Proverbs' central message, when we locate it on the road of wisdom or folly, God's way or our way, the proverb takes on a renewed practicality and power that enables its wisdom to penetrate our lives.

4. Interpret Proverbs in Cultural Context

To understand the meaning of some proverbs requires that we know about the culture and customs of the time (in this case, the tenth century before Christ) and place (Palestine). Without this information, we will sometimes miss the intensity of the proverbs' message; other times, we will miss the message completely.

Proverbs 26:17, for example, says, "Like one

who seizes a dog by the ears is a passer-by who meddles in a quarrel not his own." On the face of it, the verse's counsel appears unambiguous: Keep your nose out of other people's disputes. However, the admonition loses its force if we conceive of pulling up our pet dog by the ears. The dog won't like it, but with most pets, the puller will not be in much danger.

If we read this verse in cultural context, however, the admonition is more compelling than we first thought. Dogs were not pets in the ancient Near East, but rather wild animals, like jackals.[10] If one were to grab such a beast by the ears, the person would indeed be in jeopardy. In this light, the warning takes on a degree of urgency missing when we mentally transport Rover to 900 B.C. Proverbs 26:17 implies that one could in fact be seriously harmed by entering the fray.

In some instances, ignoring the cultural context goes beyond missing the degree of the message to entirely missing the point. In Proverbs 25 Solomon wrote, "If your enemy is hungry, give him food to eat; if he is thirsty, give him water to drink. In doing this, you will heap burning coals on his head, and the Lord will reward you" (verses 21–22). A modern reader, ignoring the cultural context, might conclude that if we are kind to our enemies, they will be injured or even devastated by the kindness. One could easily misread this as a strategy for some sort of passive retribution. But this would be erroneous, since "burning coals on his head" most likely refers to an ancient Egyptian custom of showing repentance by carrying on one's head a clay dish containing burning coals.[11] Accordingly, this proverb argues that if we are kind to our enemies, they may repent of their ways. Without knowledge of the culture to which this proverb was originally addressed, however, the reader cannot properly apply this wisdom.

5. Interpret Proverbs as Probabilities, Not Certainties

In his widely cited work *An Introduction to the Poetic Books of the Old Testament*, C. Hassell Bullock wrote that the proverbs are not "legal guarantees from God" but instead "guidelines for good behavior."[12] Similarly, in his treatise on principles of interpreting Scripture, noted author and professor Grant Osborne has written that "by their very nature [the proverbs] are generalized statements, intended to give advice rather than to establish codes by which God works."[13]

In interpreting the many promises of Proverbs, then, one should remain mindful that these are pithy nuggets of wisdom written to be memorable. Proverbs should not be construed as a rigid and contractual business manual. Rather, it offers advice that leads to a greater likelihood of human-relations success—on and off the job—for those who adopt and follow its edicts.

THE GOAL

The goal in *Management by Proverbs* is to spotlight those principles of human relations found in this practical Book of Proverbs and show how managers and organizations can tailor those proverbs to their particular needs. I will use the five interpretive guidelines above to illuminate the many selected proverbs and then apply the

meaning to the workplace. As we consider their
application, we will often look at how the teaching has succeeded at a specific organization. Like
most business innovations, many organizations
have intuitively implemented components of
proverbial management for years, albeit without
formally labeling these initiatives as such. Indeed, the advice available through Proverbs has
been road tested, and we will tap practitioners'
experiences with it for insight into implementation issues and likely outcomes.

Furthermore, many chapters will go beyond
case studies and best practices to dovetail the
findings of empirical research on employee-
management practices.

As we identify and illustrate each principle, I
believe it will become clear that *managing by
Proverbs is* not so much a novel paradigm as it is
*a transcendent approach that may simultaneously
honor God and fortify one's employee-management
system.*

THE PRINCIPAL BENEFICIARY

When God offered Solomon whatever he
wished (see 1 Kings 3:5), the new king of Israel
responded with humility:

*Now, O Lord my God, you have made your ser-
vant king in place of my father David. But I am
only a little child and do not know how to carry
out my duties. Your servant is here among the
people you have chosen, a great people, too numerous to count or number. So give your servant a discerning heart to govern your people
and to distinguish between right and wrong. For*

who is able to govern this great people of yours?"
(1 Kings 3:7–9)

The request pleased God, who granted Solomon "a wise and discerning heart" (and riches and honor as well; see 1 Kings 3:10–13). God richly blessed Solomon with the insight and discernment that is so often elusive in our own lives. By extension, though, anyone who studies the written record of this ancient partnership, largely preserved in the book of Proverbs, can share in this blessing. Through careful interpretation of the book's instruction, one gains access to a system of time-honored human-relations principles that is not available through any amount of schooling or life experience. When consistently applied in the workplace, this system has the power not only to generate a competitive advantage that is difficult to replicate, but also to do so while genuinely improving the quality of life for all who participate in that system. In the context of management theory, therefore, managing by Proverbs can be construed as an ethical grid whose benefits can accrue to both subordinates and the organization as a whole.

However, the principal beneficiary of this approach is the manager who earnestly examines, contemplates, and implements Proverbs' instruction. Indeed, many things about this person may change because, beyond being an ethical model, the book of Proverbs is a tool for intellectual growth and personal sanctification with God.

Proverbs offers the acquisition of knowledge disdained in business school and overlooked in management training programs. But it offers much more—more than the perpetual bestowal of "boss of the year" honors or the ability to think beyond the suffocating constraints of corporate culture. God's standing invitation to dine at wisdom's table offers every manager the opportunity to pursue and ultimately reach the next level of both business acumen and spiritual development.

NOTES

1. Robert Frey, "The Empowered and the Glory: A Firm's Turbulent Turnaround," *The Washington Post*, 26 December 1993, H1.
2. For a useful treatment of Ford's system, see Stephen Meyer III, *The Five Dollar Day: Labor, Management, and Social Control in the Ford Motor Company, 1908–1921* (New York: State Univ. of New York, 1981); for the initial thinking on Rockefeller's approach, see John D. Rockefeller Jr., "Labor and Capital—Partners," *The Atlantic Monthly*, January 1916, 12–21.
3. See, for example, Jeffrey Pfeffer, *Competitive Advantage Through People* (Cambridge, Mass: Harvard Business School Press, 1996); U.S. Department of Labor, *High Performance Work Practices* (Washington: D. C.: Government Printing Office, 1993); and Mark Huselid, "The Impact of Human Resource Management Practices on Turnover, Productivity and Corporate Financial Performance," *Academy of Management Journal*, 38:3 (1995): 635–72.
4. Ken Blanchard and Terry Waghorn, *Mission Possible: Becoming a World-Class Organization While There's Still Time* (New York: McGraw-Hill, 1997), 55.
5. Peter Drucker, "How to Make People Decisions," *Harvard Business Review*, July–August 1985, 54.
6. Charles R. Swindoll, gen. ed., *The Living Insights Study Bible* (Grand Rapids: Zondervan, 1996), 632. Swindoll is president of Dallas Theological Seminary.
7. Compiled and adapted from Roy B. Zuck, "A Theology of Proverbs," in Roy B. Zuck, ed., *Learning from the Sages: Selected Studies on the Book of Proverbs* (Grand

Rapids, Mich: Baker, 1995),107–110; the text first appeared in "A Theology of the Wisdom Books and the Song of Songs," in Roy B. Zuck, ed., *A Biblical Theology of the Old Testament* (Chicago: Moody, 1991), 240–42.

8. John Bright, *A History of Israel*, 3rd ed. (Louisville, Kent.: Westminster Press, 1981), 214.

9. See, for example, Brevard Childs, *Introduction to the Old Testament as a Scripture* (Minneapolis: Fortress, 1979), 552–55.

10. Greg W. Parsons, "Guidelines for Understanding and Proclaiming the Book of Proverbs," in Roy B. Zuck, ed., *Learning from the Sages*, 161.

11. Peter Cotterell and Max Turner, *Linguistics and Biblical Interpretation* (Downers Grove, Ill.: InterVarsity, 1991), 192.

12. C. Hassell Bullock, *An Introduction to the Poetic Books of the Old Testament* (Chicago: Moody, 1988), 162.

13. Grant Osborne, *The Hermeneutical Spiral* (Downers Grove, Ill.: InterVarsity, 1996), 195.

PART ONE

LAYING A PERSONAL FOUNDATION FOR SUCCESS

DEVOTE YOUR WORK TO THE REAL BOSS

In 1946, Truett Cathy, a young and ambitious entrepreneur, took out a small loan to open a restaurant in Hapeville, Georgia. The Dwarf Grill consisted of a mere ten counter seats and four tables, but the tireless Cathy steadily grew the business by serving up quality food and friendly service twenty-four hours a day, six days a week.

In this modest setting, Cathy experimented with faster ways to prepare chicken and creative ways to season it. By 1963, his persistence paid huge dividends as he developed the winning taste combination that would come to be known as the Chick-fil-A sandwich. Business took off and within a few short years, Cathy was pioneering in-mall fast food, peddling his novel sandwich to the rave reviews of hungry shoppers.

But Truett Cathy, for all of his culinary and marketing genius, did have a bit of a quirk. As a devout Christian, Cathy had refused to operate on Sundays ever since he opened the Dwarf Grill. At first, this posed little problem for his new firm. Although the policy occasionally created difficulty securing mall contracts, his recipe was in such demand that the malls simply could not say no. Fifteen years later, Chick-fil-A annual sales would top $100 million.

And then came the economic threat that would test Cathy's faith. During the deep recession of 1982, sharply lower demand for dining out caused Chick-fil-A sales to decline for the first time ever. Compounding the problem, the national burger chains suddenly became direct competitors with Cathy, offering chicken sandwiches as menu mainstays. If this were not enough, chicken prices were soaring and the company was beset with heavy debt (with interest rates hovering around 21 percent) for building a five-story office complex.[1] Financial crisis, it seemed, was imminent.

Here at the crossroads lay the specter of what had been nonnegotiable for decades: opening on the Sabbath. Adding one day of operation—especially a day where mall traffic was so high— would add at least 16 percent to current revenues. A policy change might therefore mean the difference between the mall's center court and the government's bankruptcy court.

Profitable solutions . . . God's will. Often they intersect, sometimes they do not. And it is in this latter tension that the Christian manager's faith is ultimately tested in the divine crucible. Cathy's dilemma revolved around maintaining a profit while honoring God by doing what he believed was God's will. Both those in senior management and in supervisory roles often must choose whether what they learned in business school must always come first or take second when it clashes with God's guidelines.

In effect, one must weigh the promises of the corporate culture against the promises of Scripture. And it is here that top management must decide whether the organization's direction will be charted using God's compass or a gauge of their own creation.

A PROVERB IDENTIFYING THE REAL CEO

In any situation of uncertainty, we usually choose to fall back on our own wisdom. This becomes all the more likely as the stakes escalate. However, it is for precisely such moments—the times when we are most likely to depend on our instincts, the times when we are most prone to invoke the "business-reality" rationale for compromising our faith—that Proverbs 16:3 was written:

Commit to the Lord whatever you do, and your plans will succeed.
(Proverbs 16:3)

Proverb 16:3 contains a basic biblical principle. All of the work that we do in life, indeed every endeavor we pursue, is ultimately to be performed for the glory of God.

In the New Testament, the principle is presented most directly in Paul's familiar words to the
Colossians: "Whatever you do, work at it with all
your heart, as working for the Lord, not for men,
since you know that you will receive an inheri-
tance from the Lord as a reward. It is the Lord
Christ you are serving" (3:23–24). Proverbs 16:3
imparts the same message, albeit with a focus on
a temporal rather than an eternal incentive:
"Your plans will succeed." Sound pretty straightforward? It's not.

What plans? And in what way do they "succeed"? No one translation fully captures all the
dimensions of the proverb's promise. The New
Revised Standard and the New American Standard versions of the Scriptures, for example, read
"your plans will be established"; in the King
James version, it is our "thoughts" that are established. So what exactly is the promise of 16:3?

The instruction here can be understood as an
amalgam of these translations. When we commit
our work to the Lord—when we acknowledge
Him as the real Boss to whom we ultimately report—our perspective on what we're doing and
why we're doing it changes dramatically, as does
our potential for success. Our "thoughts" about
the purpose of our work and our "plans" to effect
that purpose are no longer shaped by our peers
or the corporate culture. Instead, our thoughts
and plans are "established" (the Hebrew means
"fixed, grounded, or firmly rooted") by God. They
become divinely anchored rather than dependent
upon circumstances. God's will now preoccupies
us, displacing former priorities of expediency,

control, promotion, power, and job satisfaction. Even pay raises and job security become lesser priorities; the choice first and foremost remains God's will.

Once this new perspective is established, the ground is made fertile for us to "succeed," not necessarily in the eyes of the world, but certainly in the eyes of God. We can succeed in our reputation, esteem, integrity, and relationships. At times, this success comes at the expense of more tangible outcomes, such as pay and promotion. Most important, though, the Christian manager succeeds in the workplace as a living testimony to the truth of the Gospel.

A TRANSFORMED PERSPECTIVE

Taken as a whole, then, Proverbs 16:3 is telling us that when we genuinely devote our work to the real Boss, over time God will transform our mind-set. He'll change the way we view management and He'll inoculate us from compromising His will on the job. Our framework for business decision making will be forever altered; a new perspective will supplant the myopic and wholly secular business paradigms we have been indoctrinated to accept. Profit will become a critical piece of the story, rather than the story itself (as noted in Principle 2). Employees now become dignified children of God, rather than a factor of production (affecting our treatment of them, as noted in Principles 5–19). All told, the Christian manager now becomes an agent of Christ before he or she is an agent of the company.

In sum, there is a radical shift away from the world's parameters and toward God's service. Our

Creator will not only inform our managerial activities and everything else we do in our organization, He will also sanctify and empower us to stay on course. This is the central promise of Proverbs 16:3.

THE DECISION AT CHICK-FIL-A

Truett Cathy did not have to be reminded of this. The truths of Proverbs and Colossians were written on his heart. Consequently, he was committed to doing things God's way, independent of the cost.

In one respect, this commitment undergirded much of his financial success. He saw firsthand that a significant overlap exists between profitable solutions and God's will. There is a common ground, an intersection of the two realms. Operating in that intersection, Cathy was industrious and his work ethic shaped the corporate culture. In that intersection, Cathy cut no corners to serve the highest quality food he could produce. As he noted, "There's always a market for the best."[2] He cared for his employees, sought to meet their many needs, and reaped the lowest turnover in the industry. All these actions he saw as honoring God by honoring his employees and customers.

Cathy had, in fact, discovered another winning recipe—a recipe for building repeat business, high market share, and employee commitment.

However, as a man of principle, Cathy knew that his no-compromise approach to honoring God must also apply to those times when profitability and God's will seemed mutually exclusive. So in the midst of Chick-fil-A's 1982 crisis, he went on retreat to strategize with his top managers. It was on this retreat that Truett Cathy rededicated his business to God and, in conjunction with his management team, crafted a new corporate mission statement: "To glorify God by being a faithful steward of all that is entrusted to us and to have a positive influence on all who come in contact with Chick-fil-A."

Consistent with this vision, Cathy remained resolute in prohibiting Sunday work. Regardless of how much revenue could be generated or what capital was required, Cathy's restaurants would remain closed on the Sabbath. Period. God's will was paramount. Cathy determined that one day of rest to obey the Fourth Commandment (Exodus 20:8–11) and let his employees attend worship at church if they desired would honor God. If God wanted this six-day-a-week operation to shut down, then that's what could and should happen, Cathy concluded.

Significantly, this story has a happy ending. Cathy's company navigated through the crisis for a year until the economy recovered and interest rates and chicken prices declined. With the addition of innovative new menu items, sales accelerated throughout the 1980s and 90s, and today Chick-fil-A boasts more than 750 locations internationally with over a half-billion dollars in annual revenue. So stable is his market position that Cathy cheerfully claims to even be helping the competition, noting that: "Some of our competitors in the malls tell me that they wouldn't have made it if we didn't close on Sundays!"

Happy endings are encouraging. But it's also important for the Christian in business to recognize that they are hardly guaranteed. As many know from painful firsthand experience, in contrast to the Truett Cathy story and contrary to what a casual reading of Proverbs 16:3 might suggest, saying yes to God on the job does not always precipitate financial or career success. Legions of marketplace Christians who have pursued God's will at the expense of colleagues' respect, career growth, and even their job or business can attest to the cold reality that unhappy endings exist too.

This, of course, is the nature of the Christian life. Applying our faith invites both triumph and trial. For those who genuinely devote their work to God, though, the challenge is to recognize that God is at work regardless of the outcome.

A CONTINUOUS TENSION

Christians experience a continuous tension on the job. Day to day, hour to hour, decision to decision, we must choose between doing things the world's way and doing things God's way.

What makes the tension particularly onerous, though, is that the tug-of-war is not waged on a level playing field: The pressures of societal and corporate culture compel us to pull uphill if we want to win this battle. As Yale law professor Stephen Carter has insightfully observed: "The consistent message of modern American society is that whenever the demands of one's religion conflict with what one has to do to get ahead, one is expected to ignore the religious demands and act . . . well . . . *rationally.*"[3]

That rings true for those in the business trenches. No one wants to be labeled "irrational," especially in the practice of management. Many believe that profit, or the "bottom line," *is* the bottom line—the major goal to which all else falls second. Any other priority is not rational. So we Christians at times "rationally" shelve our faith at work, reasoning that we can bear our crosses elsewhere.

Scripture, though, teaches us to courageously reject these cultural pressures, to be less concerned with what people will think of us, and instead, to shift our focus heavenward. Most notably in this respect, the apostle Paul wrote to the Galatian church: "Am I now trying to win the approval of men, or of God? . . . If I were still trying to please men, I would not be a servant of Christ" (Galatians 1:10).

As a faithful servant, task number one for the Christian manager is to "commit to the Lord whatever you do." All else flows from this. Our God is the real Boss, the inerrant consultant for every decision, and the immovable anchorman in this daily tug-of-war. And He promises us success (in His eyes) when we unalterably stand by our commitment to Him.

NOTES

1. "Chick-fil-A; Best Run Companies," *Restaurants and Institutions*, 99, no. 14 (29 May 1989): 52.
2. Cecile S. Holmes, "We Can Accomplish Anything," *The Houston Chronicle*, 22 June 1996, religion: 1.
3. Stephen Carter, *A Culture of Disbelief* (New York: Doubleday, 1994), 13.

REGARD PROFIT
AS A
MEANS, NOT
AN
END

By every indication, things were normal during the second shift at the Malden Mills textile plant, one of the largest employers in Lawrence, Massachusetts. But then, without warning, an explosion turned an ordinary workday into a desperate rush for survival.

"I got hit and started rolling," recalled Walter Motley, one of the thirty-three injured in the blast. "The fire, it seemed like it was all over. I just tried to make the exit."

Firefighters from forty-one towns joined in the effort to contain the blaze and rescue its victims. Emergency crews airlifted some of the most critically injured to the University of Massachusetts Medical Center. Locally, a team of more than forty doctors and technicians worked feverishly to save the lives of workers, some of whom had industrial masks melt right on their faces.

When the smoke had cleared, hundreds in Lawrence, one of the most economically blighted towns in the state, were jobless and harboring little hope for future employment. The union representing Malden employees could promise only to help workers file for unemployment benefits. Maybe they could arrange for jobs in another plant, maybe not. One thing was for sure, as one shop steward said at a union meeting a couple days after the tragedy: "There won't be any jobs here again. They say there will, but there won't."

Compounding the tragedy was its timing. The explosion occurred on December 11, leaving workers to further lament that their kids would awake on Christmas morning to find little or nothing under the tree.

On December 15, the mill's owner, Aaron Feuerstein, called the workers to assemble in a school auditorium. Most expected to hear an update on the factory and the victims, and perhaps a "get-out-there-and-find-work-where-you-can" pep talk as well. Instead, what they heard made headlines around the world. Mr. Feuerstein not only announced his intention to rebuild and rehire, but he also promised to pay all of his 2,400 employees their full salary for the next thirty days. Additionally, he would continue paying their health insurance premiums for ninety days.

At that moment, depression and hopelessness turned into pandemonium as grateful employees wildly cheered their boss, hugged one another, and sporadically shouted, "God bless you, Aaron!"

This gray-haired, seventy-year-old gentleman, a devout member of his Brookline, Massachusetts, synagogue, had become a Christmas hero.[1]

What is it that makes this story so extraordinary in the world of business? For certain, Feuerstein's unconditional generosity toward his employees (to the tune of several million dollars) stands out prominently. But there's something more as well, something invisible that will make Malden Mills a controversial case study for decades to come. Underlying Feuerstein's benevolent action is an attitude about his company's financial assets, an attitude that runs against the traditional grain of corporate philosophy.

In business school and corporate culture generally, one is inculcated to think in terms of maximum profit. Businesses are, after all, economic entities and, absent economic rationales for action, they may not remain entities for very long. By contrast, though, Aaron Feuerstein's decision reflected an alternative attitude—a mind-set that generating profit is a *critical* objective of business, but not the *primary* objective. That is, in contradiction to the profit-maximization model that permeates business pedagogy, Feuerstein conceptualized profit not as an end in itself, but as a means toward a greater end: preserving families and safeguarding the welfare of his workers.

This perspective, of course, represents a somewhat radical approach to management, and as such, it has far-ranging implications discussed throughout this book. Before we explore those implications, though, it is important to understand that this approach derives from something more than human reason, rhetoric, or experience. It is, in fact, a business philosophy of divine origin.

A PROVERBIAL PERSPECTIVE ON PROFIT

Among the myriad proverbs that teach us right thinking about money, wealth, and profit, the following verse is perhaps the most representative of God's central instruction:

Wealth is worthless in the day of wrath, but righteousness delivers from death.
(Proverbs 11:4)

Examining this from a management perspective offers us at least two important lessons. Lesson one, emanating from the first half of the proverb, is that *God has a specific perspective on money, and He calls us to embrace that same perspective.* In the final accounting of our lives, we are reminded in Proverbs 11:4, God surely will not be impressed by the amount of money we accumulated. It's "worthless" on Judgment Day. Rather, God's concern will center on how we used these resources, since ultimately they belong to Him.

Christians understand this divine financial perspective not so much from reading Proverbs 11:4 in isolation as from reading it as part of the broader biblical teaching that God owns everything. The Scripture declares, "The earth is the Lord's, and everything in it, the world, and all who live in it" (Psalm 24:1). All belongs to God. Similarly, King David prayed in 1 Chronicles 29:11 that "everything in heaven and earth is yours," and in Psalm 50, God Himself said: "For the world is mine, and all that is in it" (verse 12).

In the New Testament, Christ also makes this instruction plain in the parable of the talents (Matthew 25; Luke 19), teaching that in God's eyes, we own nothing, but are merely His stewards. The inescapable conclusion with regard to financial resources, then, is that like all else, money belongs to God and He entrusts us to manage it in a way that honors Him.

Which brings us to the issue of a firm's profits. Those who generate and manage it are answerable to more than shareholders. First and foremost, profit belongs to the Lord and, as such, it should be regarded as a means to His greater glory. That implies tithing the proceeds of a business, of course, but in some circumstances, it may also imply reinvesting in the business, giving back to the community, sharing profits with employees, and limitless other allocations. Since God is sovereign and leads us down different paths of stewardship, there is no one model here. But the critical point is that *we should embrace His perspective on money and let Him lead*. In recognition that all financial resources are God's resources, the Christian manager is called to exchange the role of profit accumulator and maximizer for the role of steward.

Lesson two instructs us there are consequences of ignoring lesson one; those consequences are implied in the contrast between *wealth* and *righteousness* in the verse. Typically, a proverb will set forth two distinct paths before us, one a God-honoring path, the other displeasing to Him. So it might be natural to assume (as some do) that since "wealth" is contrasted with "righteousness" in 11:4, the verse is teaching that wealth and money are part of the unrighteous, wicked path.

This is, however, a faulty interpretation. Scripture does not teach that having wealth is sinful per se. In fact, it celebrates profit as the likely outcome of industriousness (e.g., Proverbs 10:4; 14:23). Instead, the plain instruction of Proverbs, the Gospels, and many other Scriptures is that it is *dangerous* (not sinful) to have wealth and to pursue wealth. Lesson two for the Christian manager, then, is that *one must be cautious how one thinks about profit, because money and the pursuit of money can easily transform us.*

Jesus compared the spiritual difficulty of a rich man entering heaven to that of a camel walking through the eye of a needle (see Matthew 19:24). But Proverbs 30 described another fundamental spiritual danger for the one who seeks after money:

Give me neither poverty nor riches, but give me only my daily bread. Otherwise, I may have too much and disown you and say,
"Who is the Lord?"
(Proverbs 30:8b–9)

Adopting the mind-set of money as an end, whether consciously or unconsciously, positions one on a slippery slope toward neglect of God, the proverb says. And as one slips gradually from the peak—putting God first—one's attitude morphs from steward of money to owner of money. It's a slope that culminates in the displacement of God, in spiritual death, which brings us full circle back to Proverbs 11:4. "Righteousness delivers from death," it says. Doing things God's way—seeing wealth as God sees it—is the righteous path and keeps us from spiritual erosion.

This second lesson of Proverbs 11:4, then, is nothing less than an admonition of Christ in Old Testament form: Choose your master, God or money. One must be subordinate to the other. But as you choose, remain mindful that putting money first will hinder your lifelong spiritual journey.

THE SUCCESS OF THE SERVICEMASTER COMPANY

Biblical theory aside, we must recognize that the above exegesis begs one critical question: "Can one really stay in business in the twenty-first century if one thinks this way, that God should come before profit?" In any century, the answer is the same: If it's God's will, you can. And contemporarily, the often-cited anecdotal evidence of this comes from the ServiceMaster Company.[2]

ServiceMaster of Downers Grove, Illinois, is rapidly becoming the standard by which Christian CEOs gauge their own organizational policies and procedures. It began in 1929 when a minor league baseball player named Marion Wade started a small moth-proofing company. A devout Christian, Wade committed his enterprise to the greater glory of God, and, in 1947 he incorporated the business under the name of Service-Master (from "in service of the Master").

The business gradually expanded to carpet cleaning, building cleaning, and dozens of other services. Today ServiceMaster stands atop its industry as the dominant firm providing facilities management. It operates under brand names like Terminix, Tru-Green, ChemLawn, and Merry Maids, and its annual systemwide revenues exceeded $4 billion in 1997. What is enamoring about this particular industry leader, though, is that, through all of its growth and diversification, it has never wavered from the original vision and purpose of its founder.

ServiceMaster's mission is comprised of four pieces. In their stated order, the four are: "to honor God in all we do, to help people develop, to pursue excellence, and to grow profitably." What's even more arresting than the mission statement's "God language" (as some shareholders call it) is the interpretation of this statement by top management. According to C. William Pollard, Chairman and CEO of ServiceMaster, "The first two objectives are end goals. The second two are means goals. As we seek to implement these objectives in the operation of our business, they provide us with a reference point for seeking to do that which is right and avoiding that which is wrong."[3] That is, Pollard contends that the reason ServiceMaster exists is to honor God and to help people develop, and that profit is conceptualized as only a means to these two ends.

Well, talk is cheap. Anyone can advance a lofty

vision and blithely make overtures that support that vision. At ServiceMaster, though, the vision genuinely envelops business policy and strategy. It affects everything from how the customer is regarded (as a group of people, not as an impersonal organization) to how the organization is structured (to enable and empower those closest to the customer).[4]

ServiceMaster's "profit-as-a-means" mind-set also has considerable implications for employee management. The company vigilantly safeguards human dignity, makes a priority of training and career development, and grants employees a share in the profits and in the ownership of the firm. Managers are sensitized to the arduousness of subordinates' tasks by periodically performing those tasks. And more generally, managers operate under a servant-leadership ethic. Says Pollard on this point: "Leaders in our firm should never ask any one to do something that they are unwilling to do for themselves."[5]

Of course, many other firms with wholly secular orientations do these things as well, but significantly, ServiceMaster does so while regarding profit as a means to an end; yet it still enjoys the financial success of an industry leader. In essence, ServiceMaster demonstrates that it is possible to have it both ways—to treat profit in a God-honoring manner and to simultaneously remain profitable.

BLENDING BUSINESS PERFORMANCE WITH SCRIPTURAL MANDATES

For many on the front lines of commerce, the notion of putting something—anything—before

profit is both unwise and irresponsible. Such an-
ticompetitive paradigms, they claim, undermine
the basic tenets of capitalism, threaten the firm,
and forsake one's responsibilities to the shareholders. Business exists, the mantra resounds, to
maximize shareholder wealth.

For Christians in business, though, the question of why one is in business is superseded by
the question of why one is here. To this latter ex-
istential question, the answer is found in places
like Ecclesiastes 12:13: "Fear God and keep his
commandments, for this is the whole duty of
man." As paraphrased by firms like ServiceMaster, this means "to honor God in all we do." The
implications are enormous and daunting.

From a practical perspective, this implies that
for the Christian manager at any level, *every managerial decision should be made while considering
both business performance and scriptural mandates.*

The ideal is to accomplish both objectives.
However, this is not always possible. Situations
will inevitably arise where these two guiding paradigms directly conflict. Will you use sexy models
and lust as marketing tools? Will you gamble on
significant debt in order to expand the business?
Will you weigh an employee's family responsibilities when making compensation, promotion, and
layoff decisions? The list of scenarios where the
profit motive and God's will are mutually exclusive is limitless.

It is here where both corporate culture and our
business instincts hasten us to yield our faith.
And it is at precisely this moment, the moment of
greatest pressure to disdain Christ, where the

Christian manager sees most clearly that the way of the Cross is not always the way of maximum profit. It is here where he or she is called to make choices that are simultaneously God honoring, unpopular, and even unnatural.

This is surely no small task, since it typically requires a willingness to stand against a tidal wave of opposition, and, in many cases, to chart a complete sea change in one's own business philosophy. But the good news is that once the latter happens, the former follows naturally.

Faithfully honoring God in business begins with a transplant: We must replace our mainstream perspective on profit with God's perspective on profit. God reveals to us through His Word that profit is to be neither condemned nor idolized, but, instead, it is to be treated as God's property. The Christian manager is therefore called to consider himself or herself a steward of this resource and to regard profit as a powerful means to God's greater glory.

NOTES

1. This anecdote was compiled from the following sources: from the *Boston Globe*, Don Aucoin and Pamela Ferdinand, "In Lawrence, Hope Goes Up in Smoke," 13 December 1995, 37; Brian MacQuarrie, "Quiet Heroes Help Pick Up the Pieces," 13 December 1995, 37; Brian MacQuarrie, "Workers Recall Fire's Fury," 14 December 1995, 37; Richard Saltus, "Team Effort Saved Burn Victims," 17 December 1995, 45; and from *The Tampa Tribune*, Sandy Banisky, "Mill Boss Is No Grinch; Saves Town Christmas," 25 December 1995, 1.
2. Information on ServiceMaster comes from the Internet at www.svm.com and from the book by C. William Pollard, *The Soul of the Firm* (Grand Rapids: Zondervan, 1996).
3. Pollard, *The Soul of the Firm*, 18–19.
4. Ibid., 75, 85.
5. Ibid., 130.

BE HUMBLE

Bill Foote stood before an audience of 150 managers to deliver his first speech since becoming the chief executive officer of USG Corporation, a building products manufacturer in Chicago. But as he began, it quickly became apparent that this would be anything but the prototypical "here's-my-vision" talk.

The CEO opened by conveying a traumatic and intensely personal story. Eighteen months earlier, he had learned that his wife, Andrea, was diagnosed with breast cancer. The Footes, parents of three young girls, courageously waged an all-out battle with the disease; but one month before Bill was named CEO, Andrea died. She was only forty-two years old.

Now shouldering the new roles of widower, single parent, and chief executive, Bill Foote elected to stand before his management team emotionally exposed. He spoke from his heart.

This unusual step of publicly sharing his struggles quieted the room. "You could have heard a pin drop," said one manager. Veteran managers were wiping tears away.

The upshot of Bill's candor was equally unusual. *The Wall Street Journal* later reported that: "As managers talked afterwards, . . . the clear message was 'If we have to go through a few walls for this guy, we're going to do it.'" Additionally, Bill's willingness to demonstrate his own vulnerability and humanity reverberated throughout the organization. The company showed a renewed attentiveness to family issues and, more generally, a broader sensitivity to employee needs. For instance, when executives decided to close a Virginia plant the year after Bill's speech, workers got two and one-half years notice and ample outplacement help.

"By all accounts," concluded the *Journal*, "both Mr. Foote's leadership and the corporate culture at USG . . . emerged stronger."[1]

HOW TO RECOGNIZE HUMILITY

Humility manifests itself in several ways, as does its opposite, pride. And as poignantly illustrated by Bill Foote, one manifestation of a humble attitude is the willingness to lay bare one's afflictions, vulnerabilities, and insecurities—a willingness to share with others that one has the same human frailties that they have. In some of its other forms, humility can surface as a disposition to serve others first, as a candor about one's shortcomings, or as an inclination to welcome advice (Principle 11).

In the context of the workplace, "managerial humility" can be defined as an attitude that, notwithstanding the imparity with subordinates in title, authority, education, skill, or paycheck, *there really is no difference at the most basic level of one's existence.* That is, for the Christian manager, genuine humility means renouncing the man-made status distinctions between persons, in favor of God's more egalitarian model.

No doubt, this mind-set is unnatural to a sinful mankind permeated with pride. And it's certainly uncommon in bureaucratic organizations, where hierarchical structure accentuates and institutionalizes such status distinctions. For those who strive to be more humble as managers and those who would consider such a change, the Scriptures offer guidance. Indeed, humility is one of the most widely addressed topics in Proverbs and in Scripture generally.

PROVERBS ON HUMILITY

Among the many proverbs that speak to the issue of humility, perhaps the most eloquent is one in which the word "humility" never appears:

Rich and poor have this in common:
The Lord is Maker of them all.
(Proverbs 22:2)

No Distinctions Before God

Indeed, we all know that. God created everyone and everything. This is as basic as theology gets.

But, for some reason, the knowledge of this fundamental truth that we're all children of the same Father—all loved by Him, all valuable in His eyes—does not always migrate from one's head to one's heart. Instead, Christians, like others, tend to mentally adhere to distinctions and pecking orders that are abhorrent to a God who challenges us to see people as He sees them.

Proverbs 22:2 is an important reminder that the cornerstone of managing people in humility is to recognize that *those under us at work in fact stand next to us, where it really matters, before the Creator*. In the New Testament, the apostle Paul picks up this theme often. "Do not think of yourself more highly than you ought, but rather think of yourself with sober judgment" (Romans 12:3), he told Christians in Rome. This implies that God calls Christian managers to reject outright the elevated standing conferred on them at the managerial level. Instead, as a Christian manager, each of us should, "in humility, consider others better than yourself" (Philippians 2:3).

Humility vs. Pride: Two Distinct Paths

Beyond the basic admonition, though, Proverbs also offers us consequences, foretelling the likely result of both a humble attitude and its antithesis, a proud spirit. Consider this small but representative sampling of its instruction:

> *When pride comes, then comes disgrace, but with humility comes wisdom.*
> (Proverbs 11:2)

Pride goes before destruction,
a haughty spirit before a fall.
(Proverbs 16:18)

Before his downfall a man's heart
is proud, but humility comes
before honor.
(Proverbs 18:12)

Humility and fear of the Lord bring
wealth and honor and life.
(Proverbs 22:4)

The two paths and their destinations are distinct. Humility is a precursor to wisdom, honor, wealth, and a God-honoring life, whereas pride precipitates disgrace, destruction, and one's downfall. Many may already sense pride's outcome, since most of us have made these sorts of missteps and experienced pride's troubling results. However, the outcomes of humility are less obvious and warrant some closer inspection, particularly in a managerial context.

HUMILITY AND PRIDE
IN EMPLOYEE MANAGEMENT

On a practical level, the ramifications of adopting an attitude of humility touch almost every aspect of employee management. From staffing to performance management to the severing of the employment relation, one's ability to make Christlike decisions is largely a function of one's willingness to adopt the role of servant and put others' needs ahead of one's own. By contrast, decisions that are fueled by one's pride tend to be decisions that are displeasing to God and not beneficial to employees.

In addition, our attitudes as managers in reaching decisions can affect our efficiency and productivity in our unit, and prideful attitudes can invade most areas of management. Table 3 provides a cross section of the manifestations of a prideful versus a humble attitude.

Table 3

PRIDE VERSUS HUMILITY IN EMPLOYEE MANAGEMENT

Issue	Prideful Attitude	Humble Attitude
Interviewing Applicants	I can ascertain what I need to know about people from speaking to them.	A second opinion and maybe an employment test would be helpful.
Employee Career Development	That's the employee's job, not mine.	I have a responsibility to make this a priority.
Soliciting Employee Ideas	I know more than they do. Meritorious ideas from below make me look less valuable.	I can learn from the people on the front lines. This organization can benefit from their perspectives.
Relieving Employee Stress	I've got enough to do without worrying about their stress level.	It's part of my job to improve quality of work life.
Employee Family Obligations	If I accommodate this request, I'll have to accommodate every other employee as well.	Who am I to undermine their families?

ISSUE	PRIDEFUL ATTITUDE	HUMBLE ATTITUDE
Dealing with Under-performers	Improve or we'll have to take some other action.	Has management contributed to the under-performance? Regardless, can I do something to help this person improve?
Conflict Resolution	I'm the sole and final arbiter of conflicts. This maintains control and consistency.	I may overlook something or have a latent bias, so there needs to be an objective system in place to safeguard due process.
Overall	I'm the boss.	God's the Boss.

These prideful responses may seem harsh, yet at times we all tend toward them on one or more of these issues. In contrast, consider the tone behind the humble response. It should be clear that humility can lead to things like honor, wealth, wisdom, and a vibrant spiritual life. The manager who humbly meets employee needs in such realms as career development, participation, job satisfaction, family time, training, and due process will be highly revered, perhaps "honored" above other managers in the organization. Moreover, as we will see throughout this book, empirical and anecdotal evidence indicate that displaying a humble attitude leads to greater employee commitment, productivity, and retention, as well as better quality and organizational performance. Stated differently, humility can lead to "wealth" through these mediating variables.

It also can lead to wisdom, for the willingness to learn from others and bring others into the decision-making process (as with interviewing applicants, to cite one of many possible examples) can advance one's knowledge and insight. This linkage between humility and wisdom is highlighted in Principle 11, valuing employee input (by both soliciting employee ideas and taking advice; see pages 162–167).

Overall, having the humility to defer to God as the head of the organization and to acknowledge that He knows better than we what's best for our organization, brings "life" to our relationship with Him. To recapitulate a point from Principle 1, all else flows from devoting one's work to the One who created work.

Indeed, as Proverbs 22:4 teaches, "Humility and the fear of the Lord bring wealth and honor and life."

EMBRACING HUMILITY

Few attitudes are further removed from Christ's model than an inflated sense of one's own importance or stature. Christ is the very embodiment of humility, for He "made himself nothing, taking the very nature of a servant." He was God, but for our sins "he humbled himself and became obedient to death—even death on a cross" (Philippians 2:7–8). Our task, Paul wrote, is to emulate this example: "Your attitude should be the same as that of Christ Jesus" (Philippians 2:5).

In our workplace fiefdoms, then, whether it be atop a multibillion-dollar company like USG Corp. or leading an eight-member team in a work unit, Christian managers through word and deed are called to bear witness to the humility of Christ. This entails a willingness to serve rather than to be served (Matthew 20:28), a contentment in being second rather than first, a greater propensity to listen than desire to be heard, and a teachability that permits us to learn from those around us. Furthermore, embracing humility in one's career is to view ourselves quite differently —"with sober judgment" as Paul put it in Romans 12:3. It is to see one's good works as works of God, one's accomplishments as really His accomplishments, one's talents as His gifts, and one's good fortune as His providence.

In total, a humble manager can see himself (herself) and others from God's perspective, not man's. As humble managers, we can see more clearly our relative smallness, despite whatever power or position God has granted us. We are less likely to think too much of ourselves, to allow our innate pride to subvert God's plan for our work.

Lastly, in managing our people, seeing through God's eyes inhibits us from drifting toward thinking autocratically (with all of its harmful consequences). Instead, we recognize that despite any educational or experiential advantage we have on those under us, we are, in fact, not superior to them where it matters most: before God. "The Lord," the proverb reminds us, "is Maker of them all."

NOTE

1. Sue Shellenbarger, "A CEO Opens Up About Loss and Finds He's a Stronger Boss," *The Wall Street Journal,* 10 September 1997, B1.

PRINCIPLE FOUR

PRIORITIZE FAMILY
OVER
WORK

I've struggled with this for a long time," said Brenda Barnes, a twenty-two-year veteran employee of PepsiCo, the parent company of Pepsi-Cola. Brenda, the mother of three children, ages seven, eight, and ten, had spent more than half her life climbing the corporate ladder. Now, nearing the top wrung, she held the titles of president and CEO of Pepsi's North American division. At age forty-three, Brenda was among the highest-ranking women in corporate America, controlling an operation that reported about $1.4 billion in annual profits, and drawing a paycheck of nearly $2 million a year. [1]

But her ascension and impressive stature came at a significant price. To be a central player in top management required regular dinner meetings and a hectic travel schedule. Most workdays spanned an exhausting sixteen hours—from 3:30 A.M. to 7:30 P.M.—affording her only a few daily minutes with her family. Brenda was missing most of her sons' football games. She saw school plays only via videotape. And when a child's birthday fell on a weekday, Mom was conspicuously absent.

Brenda's long struggle illustrates a tension that all working parents experience to various degrees. We seek to offer 100 percent to both work life and family life, but seldom succeed. Inevitably, something suffers, and often it is our family: our spouse and/or the children. The family gets short shrift, dominated by the seemingly urgent needs of the workplace.

Conventional wisdom suggests that the work-family tension is caused by business realities that are simply beyond our control. Consider the nature of managerial and professional positions. Some require travel; there's no way around it. Many require long hours for deadlines and pressing projects. And in an increasingly competitive environment, one is often compelled to stay at work into the dinner hour, regardless of one's personal situation. After all, who can really tell a prospective client: "Sorry, you can keep your $50,000 because I promised to meet my kid's teacher this afternoon"? Some positions even require weekend work if one has any aspiration of advancing. That's the inescapable corporate norm.

Even when a profit motive does not exist, there are similar pressures to trade off family for work. Ask any charity director who's soliciting contributions full-time just to keep the charity afloat. Or inquire with a church pastor about the last time he worked a mere forty-hour week. I assure you, it was prior to seminary.

So this is what it's come to at the turn of the millennium: Our culture has now evolved to a point where career success (or sometimes just career maintenance) demands more personal commitment and flexibility on our part than ever before. The culprit, we reason, is the nature of business, these unalterable realities. The casualty is our family time.

PROVERBS' UNCONVENTIONAL WISDOM

So says the conventional wisdom. And occasionally it has some merit. Proverbs, however, offers a less fatalistic perspective. It suggests that the work-family dilemma may often be more a function of things internal to ourselves than of situations beyond our control. It does not point to others, such as an overtaxing boss or demanding employees or deadlines, but to our own ambition, our pride, and, in some cases, our greed.

Ask Why

Accordingly, Proverbs' unconventional wisdom calls us to be introspective, regularly and candidly scrutinizing *why* we're pursuing this particular career path, *why* we're working so many hours, and *why* we're taking so many responsibilities. Is the reason something elemental like job security, or are there some nefarious motivators underlying it? Is the reason simply the need to put food on the table and save for the kids' college, or is it more the pursuit of luxuries, a title, prestige, and power?

Proverbs 23:4–5 assists us in distinguishing our legitimate from illegitimate reasons for working long hours:

Do not wear yourself out to get rich; have the wisdom to show restraint. Cast but a glance at riches, and they are gone, for they will surely sprout wings and fly off to the sky like an eagle.

The first admonition is reasonably straightforward. The pursuit of riches is not worthy of our limited time and energy. But *riches* does not refer solely to money. Throughout the Old Testament, the word translated here as *rich* and *riches* also carries the connotation of accumulation or enrichment. The broader implication? We should not wear ourselves out to accumulate possessions or to enrich ourselves with power, adulation, or other ego fodder. Rather, we are to pursue a different path.

Wisdom's path is one of "restraint," but not just a passive restraint. We are to be active and urgent. The *New Revised Standard Version*, for example, translates this as "be wise enough to desist"; the *New American Standard Bible* and King James Version tell us to cease from our own wisdom, our current consideration of chasing wealth and other riches.

Beyond simply exercising restraint, then, the proverb's author is alerting us to a tendency to make idols of career and accumulation, and he tells us to desist now. Do not follow the path that is innate to you, "thine own wisdom," as it says in the King James Version. Resist the temptation. Even if you do find the enrichment for which you exhaust yourself, it will be fleeting, we are told in 23:5; it will ultimately "fly off."

Watch Out for Personal Desire

This point is critical. Following our own inclinations—the sinful nature that is inherent to the human condition—ultimately destroys us. It inhibits our relationship with God and erodes our relationship with our family. We see this same instruction even more clearly in Proverbs 5. In the midst of a long discourse on adultery and repeated warnings against pursuing our carnal lusts, Solomon warned, "Drink water from your own cistern" and "rejoice in the wife of your youth" (verses 5:15, 18). The teaching is that it may seem natural to succumb to lust because of how you are designed. You will be tempted. But "cease and desist!" Show restraint, turn from your consideration of it, and rejoice in your family. Follow God's path rather than your own.

Thus, as we wrestle with balancing work and family, we should remember the innate, ever-present temptation to subordinate family needs to personal desires. It matters not whether those desires be power, or material objects, or bragging rights, or a level of affirmation not currently available at home. Proverbs challenges us to vigilantly resist the drift toward pursuing these riches at the expense of family.

Notice that this is an *internal* issue. The tension we experience has little to do with the nature of business; rather, Proverbs implicates the sinful nature of man as the primary culprit. For any individual, the tension may be precipitated by a natural tendency to pursue one's own definition of success rather than God's definition. In this light, then, Proverbs invites us to consider whether any work-family imbalance can be remedied from within.

THE BENEFITS OF KEEPING FAMILY FIRST

The Benefits to the Family

Elsewhere in Proverbs, we are apprised of the familial consequences of choosing between the paths of wisdom and folly. Here is a telling juxtaposition:

> *The righteous man leads a*
> *blameless life; blessed are*
> *his children after him.*
> (Proverbs 20:7)

> *A greedy man brings trouble*
> *to his family, but he who hates*
> *bribes will live.*
> (Proverbs 15:27)

In both verses, we see that how we live our lives affects the members of our household. There are many consequences of righteous living, and among them, as noted in Proverbs 20:7, is a blessing for our children. They are prime beneficiaries when we walk God's path, when we faithfully do things like ranking family before career.

But this outcome operates in the negative direction as well. The "greedy" man in 15:27, one who "profits illicitly" (NASB), one who is "greedy for unjust gain" (NRSV), brings trouble to his household. The linkage is explicit and inescapable. If we covet the big bucks and the corner office, and if we use every means at our disposal to get them, we run a tremendous risk back home. Whether we're in the boardroom or on the assembly line, leading a company, leading a charity, or leading a revival, Proverbs' message is the same. The path of folly is expensive beyond measure. Prioritize family over work.

The Benefits to the Organization

Clearly, aligning personal priorities in this manner pays personal dividends. But what about its effect on the management system? For the organization, is there any value added when a boss thinks in terms of family first?

One might speculate that a work group would be hamstrung by having a person at the top who embraces other priorities first. But in practice, this person will be more asset than liability for the group and the organization as a whole. Here's why.

From a strictly financial perspective, a family-sensitive manager serves not only employee needs but can meet long-term organizational objectives better than the traditional work-first manager can. The mushrooming corporate initiatives in this area powerfully testify to this truth. Many larger employers have seen the wisdom of including benefits like health and life insurance, employee assistance programs, dependent-care spending accounts, and college scholarships among their employee benefits. Others also have engaged in work redesign, developing flexible work arrangements, telecommuting, and job sharing as business policy-makers recognize the value of lowering tensions both in the employee's work and family life.

As much as we'd like to think that these trends are a function of a more enlightened, more ethical, and even more compassionate boardroom, much of the movement owes its impetus to the profit motive. "Family-friendly" work environments can be good for business. In fact, this notion is becoming so accepted that popular periodicals such as *Business Week* and *Fortune*, publications that target the traditional, profit-minded manager, are now generating biannual surveys to coronate the top family-friendly employers.

So a linkage seems to exist between sensitivity to employee family concerns and organizational performance. But there's an important element to remember here. Regardless of the extent of a company's family-friendly policies, *the value of family-sensitive management ultimately depends on how individual bosses respond to individual employee needs*. This is why the boss who personally embraces the primacy of family is such an asset to the organization: He or she is more likely to genuinely satisfy those pressing employee concerns, thereby nurturing a covenant that engenders commitment, productivity, and long-term retention.

PUTTING FAMILY FIRST

Putting family ahead of work requires both humility and faith. It is a selfless act that may entail the humble decision to relinquish some work responsibilities, to pass up a promotion, or to step off the fast track. Even more radically, it might mean changing jobs altogether or possibly leaving the security of a salaried position to open up your own shop from home. For one who is already an entrepreneur, it might mean cutting back hours by taking on a partner. Note that a residual consequence in many of these scenarios will be accepting a pay cut in the faith that God will provide.

Note also there are no cookie-cutter answers here. Prognoses will vary with individual circumstances. For Brenda Barnes, though, the struggle gave way to a decision that many adherents to the conventional wisdom would find unthinkable.

"I've struggled with this for a long time," she told Pepsi and the rest of the world. But "the time has come for me to devote 100 percent of my time to them." The "them" in her statement was her husband and children. Brenda had elected to step down from her position as a captain of industry, to give up her seven-figure salary, and to suspend her professional career in favor of being a stay-at-home mom.

Pepsi's top brass pulled out all the stops to dissuade her. They offered a more flexible schedule, fewer responsibilities, less demanding jobs. Even their legendary former chairman Donald Kendall got involved. Pepsi had been grooming Brenda "for bigger things," they said, and would do whatever it took to keep her.

Brenda talked it over with her family. What would it take to strike a better balance? Among the possible resolutions, one of her children offered that she could keep working if she'd promise to be home for all of their birthdays. For Brenda, that clinched it. When your grade-school children are asking for just a few days of your time between now and when they leave for college, it's time to make some tough choices, she concluded.[2]

Other struggles have similarly culminated in relinquishing vast "riches" for the sake of family. In the 1990s, Robert Reich left his position as secretary of labor for family reasons; Peter Lynch, head of Fidelity's hugely profitable Magellan Fund, did the same. Penny Hughes, another beverage executive, gave up her position as Coca-Cola president for Great Britain and Ireland, all for her baby.[3]

The Book of Proverbs does not mandate that we, in the name of the family, must leave the workforce or find a new job. But it does remind us that the work-related choices we make are in fact choices, and that they will have a profound effect on our relationships at home. Moreover, it counsels us about how easy it is to make the wrong work-family choices, to surrender to the temptations of our nature. If we do so, we in effect sacrifice children and marriage at the altar of career success. To avoid this, Proverbs invites us to map our priorities to God's priorities, fitting career into a nonnegotiable family schedule, rather than the other way around.

NOTES

1. David Roeder, "CEO Picks Family Over Job," *Chicago Sun-Times*, 25 September 1997, 3.

2. Dottie Enrico, "Pepsi Chief Trades Work for Family," *USA Today,* 25 September 1997, 3B.
3. Mrs. Hughes gave her reasons to English journalists; like her counterpart, Brenda Barnes at PepsiCo headquarters, Hughes desired greater involvement with her children. See James Bone and Joanna Bale, "Pepsi Chief Quits to Watch Her Boys Play Football," *The Times of London,* 25 September 1997, 1.

PART TWO

BUILDING
A
COMPETITIVE
WORKFORCE

MEASURE TWICE, HIRE ONCE

Working the late shift, Ronny Quynn had just stepped outside for a cigarette break when out from the bushes sprang several masked men. Brandishing handguns, they roughed up Ronny, taped his eyes shut, and demanded he give them access to The Cyrix Corporation's facility. Ronny had little choice. Using his security badge, he led the men through several locked doors and into Cyrix's manufacturing area where workers assembled the company's valuable computer chips.

The bandits tied up four other employees and forced them to lie on the ground. They then proceeded to swipe as many computer chips as they could carry. In a matter of minutes, the $350,000 heist—the largest of its kind in 1994—was complete.

The police later charged five members of a local gang with the robbery. According to an informant from the gang, the thieves "had inside information which would make the robbery easier to accomplish." In fact, the gang had infiltrated Cyrix by placing one of its own as an employee.[1]

The Cyrix saga is not unique. According to the Society for Human Resource Management, gang members are increasingly passing themselves off as legitimate job applicants, not only to gain access to merchandise, but also for health insurance and other benefits.[2] And it's not just callow personnel managers being duped. Gang members have even navigated the elaborate screening process of the Chicago Police Department.[3]

Poor hiring decisions are both costly and commonplace. A classic case, studied in most employment law courses, involved the hiring of a trucker who, unbeknownst to the company, was a convicted rapist. Within days on the job, this formerly incarcerated new employee had picked up and raped a hitchhiker.[4]

Labor unions, too, have mastered the fine art of applicant deception. For many years, they have used a legal[5] and extremely effective tactic known as "salting," in which union organizers apply for rank-and-file positions in nonunion companies. Once inside, the organizer stands a much greater chance of both reaching employees with the union's message and securing a representation election.

Of course, it's not only polished con artists who misrepresent their background to prospective employers. A 1988 study of two hundred job applicants by Equifax, a nationwide background-checking firm, concluded that 29 percent of these applicants lied on their résumés about dates of employment, 11 percent lied about reasons for leaving previous jobs, and 8 percent exaggerated their amount of schooling.[6] More recently, a 1994 survey by AccounTemps similarly concluded that about one-third of résumés contain misrepresentations of employment histories, degrees, and other vital information.[7]

PROVERBS ON STAFFING

Take a Serious Approach to Staffing

Indeed, employee selection is a more precarious task than ever. Or is it? The Book of Proverbs illustrates an ancient familiarity with the pitfalls of staffing, specifically cautioning us against any casual approach to measuring applicant qualifications and integrity. One key verse is directly on target:

---

*Like an archer who wounds
at random is he who hires
a fool or any passer-by.*
(Proverbs 26:10)

The "archer" Solomon referred to was not a leisurely hunter. Archers in biblical times were highly skilled warriors. Trained from childhood and deadly accurate, they were an army's first line of attack because they could neutralize the enemy from great distances. Little could prevent them from completing their task since, in addition to their pinpoint precision, their arrows could pierce almost any type of contemporary armor.

Now consider what is implied by an archer

who wounds at random, or, as translated in the *New Revised Standard Version* (NRSV) and the *New American Standard Bible*, an archer who wounds everyone. This individual's performance is commensurate with neither his training nor the acumen of his peers. He is exceptionally bad at something that he should be doing exceptionally well. Moreover, he's a risk. An archer who wounds at random sometimes wounds allies. He is worse than unproductive; he is counterproductive since he shoots people on his own side and undermines the war effort.

It would seem, then, that in choosing this simile, Solomon was making the general observation that *an informal approach to hiring is careless and perilous*. It amounts to doing something poorly that needs to be performed incisively. When it is not, the process harms at random. No stakeholder is immune, from the firm's owners to the hiree's supervisor to his coworkers, or from the new employee's internal and external customers to the new employee himself, who is mismatched to the job.

Consider the Applicant's Character

The proverb also offers more specific instruction: We should hire neither "fools" nor just "any passer-by." What is translated here as "fool" is not the same word from Proverbs 1:7 that carries a connotation of moral deficiency (see introductory chapter); rather, the word more closely describes those who are arrogant, silly, or simple. And what is translated here as proscribing the hire of "any passer-by" can also mean, more narrowly, don't hire drunkards (in fact, that is the translation in both the NRSV and the Bible in Basic English). One could therefore infer a further message from Proverbs 26:10: Employee character matters, and we should measure it before extending any job offers.

Elsewhere in Proverbs, this advice about applicant character is advanced even more directly, as illustrated by the following tandem of verses:

As vinegar to the teeth and smoke to the eyes, so is a sluggard to those who send him.
(Proverbs 10:26)

Like the coolness of snow at harvest time is a trustworthy messenger to those who send him; he refreshes the spirit of his masters.
(Proverbs 25:13)

In Proverbs 10:26, we again see the negative consequences of a hiring error. The boss who hires a "sluggard" reaps nothing but discomfort. Indeed, he gets burned (as smoke might burn the eyes) and becomes embittered (as vinegar is bitter to the teeth). If he had instead employed someone reliable and industrious, a "trustworthy messenger," he might have been refreshed. That is, his burden would have been lightened rather than exacerbated. The chasm between these two outcomes should prod the manager to staff judiciously and, as part of that staffing process, to consider character traits (such as the prospective hiree's work ethic and trustworthiness).

CALIBRATING THE SELECTION SYSTEM

These proverbs encourage what businesspeople may know intuitively, but for various reasons sometimes disregard: A staffing system should be sophisticated enough to accurately and consistently screen out undesirable applicants. And the measurement of character, as difficult as it may be, should be a focal point in the system.

The design of an effective staffing system begins with knowing what it is one needs to measure. In human resource parlance, this often-neglected step is called conducting a "job analysis" for the vacant position or, from a macro perspective, for each job in the organization. In a sentence, the job analysis identifies (1) all of the specific tasks performed in the job, and (2) the knowledge, skills, abilities, and other attributes (like character) required to successfully perform these tasks. Typically, more formal approaches to job analysis generate better data than less formal ones.[8]

Once we identify exactly what is to be measured, the screening phase usually includes some combination of reference checking, employment tests, and personal interviews. Each of these elements acts as a gauge, however imperfect, of the prospective qualifications and future job performance. To refine the metrics for our current hiring processes, we can benefit from using all three tools, provided we recognize and address their limitations.

Reference Checking

Every employer asks for references. They not only serve as an important check on data given by the applicant; they often provide information that is simply unavailable through any other means.

Of course, this assumes you will be able to get the information from the references. It seems that people just won't talk about former employees anymore. However, the trend is not borne of a fresh respect for scriptural teachings on gossip. Like so many current people-management initiatives, it is driven by a concern over man's law.

In particular, defamation suits—allegations that Person A harmed Person B's reputation by communicating something to Person C—have prompted a steadily increasing number of organizations to prohibit their employees from granting references. As a result, when checking references, the best you can get much of the time are the dates of employment, eligibility for re-hire, and the title of the position this person held. They can't tell you that the guy was terminated for sexually harassing a coworker. It's company policy.

A 1995 survey affords us some insight into the magnitude of the problem. According to the Society for Human Resource Management, among 1,331 responding human resource professionals, 63 percent said that they or a staff member has refused to provide information about a former employee due to fear of a lawsuit, and 17 percent said they had actually been challenged by a disgruntled former employee alleging that an inaccurate reference had been furnished.[9] Reference checking, historically a staple for soliciting critical information, is fast becoming a bankrupt enterprise. The law has rendered reference providers mute.[10] Consequently, employment tests and personal interviews must pick up this slack.

Employment Tests

The growth of testing instruments developed during the past two decades gives testimony to deficiencies in other selection tools. Employment tests purport to predict things like applicant Smith's cognitive ability, his job skills, his leadership potential, and his illicit drug use from this past weekend. They'll forecast for you whether Smith is emotionally stable or if he instead might come to work toting an AK-47. Does he have a propensity to steal or is he so uncompromisingly honest that he'll turn in his own mother for pilfering a girdle?

For most business professionals, the legitimacy and value of things like performance tests or cognitive exams is a settled issue. We generally believe, and rightly so, that these instruments deliver on their claims of validity. What is less certain, though, is the validity of tests that probe dimensions of an applicant's character. Such tools are often perceived as transparent in what they seek and, therefore, fakable. After all, what applicant is going to offer a self-depreciating response to the question: "Have you ever stolen from your employer?"

However, testing instruments for these intangibles have evolved rapidly in recent years. And in the scholarly community, there has been no lack of zeal for scrutinizing their accuracy. We can report that those studies have shown some employment tests can indeed effectively assess character. To date, research appearing in top management and applied psychology journals has affirmed the validity of both honesty tests[11] and other "organizational delinquency" tests (appraising the likelihood for vandalism, absenteeism, grievances, insubordination, violence, etc.).[12] Moreover, recent large-sample studies have concluded that test-taker attempts to distort answers are not much of a threat to these tests' validity.[13] In other words, some of the sensitive character data that, according to Proverbs, is a prerequisite for making wise staffing decisions can be gathered through employment tests.

But remember, the adage "you get what you pay for" is never more applicable than it is here. There are plenty of bargain-basement tests out there that measure nothing but one's ability to take that test. So carefully research character tests before you buy them. Take them yourself to evaluate their predictive capabilities. Then, invest in one of the better ones. In doing so, you will procure a powerful tool for raising red flags where they should be raised and for directing attention to applicants who may have otherwise been overlooked.

Personal Interviews

What organization does not rely on the interview? It is without question the tool of choice in employee selection, being accorded more weight than any other.[14]

But this is usually a mistake, and a significant one at that. It is precisely our overreliance on the personal interview that is responsible for both re-

grettable hiring decisions and the untold rejec-
tions of those who would have been exceptional
workers. We interviewers pride ourselves on being accomplished predictors of ability and judges
of character and therefore give controlling
weight to the twenty minutes we spend with a
person. Indeed, much of the time, we make what
later seems to be the right call; other times this is
not the case.

The Book of Proverbs suggests that a person
has an infinite capacity to mislead, and that we
should weigh interviews more lightly than we do:

---

*A malicious man disguises
himself with his lips, but in
his heart he harbors deceit.
Though his speech is charming,
do not believe him, for seven
abominations fill his heart.
His malice may be concealed
by deception, but his wickedness
will be exposed in the assembly.*
(Proverbs 26:24–26)

Regardless of our experience, we can still be
hoodwinked. If we naively or stubbornly ignore
this possibility, we'll probably make more staffing
mistakes than if we humbly acknowledge it.

Moreover, the proverb teaches that when we do
make such a mistake, the blunder will ultimately
become public information. In King Solomon's
day, an "assembly" referred to a gathering of

many people, usually at an appointed time (not unlike the contemporary workplace). Part of the proverb's message, then, is that whereas an individual may be able to initially conceal his persona, over time, and among many people, the truth about him will become evident. On the job, his character flaws will eventually be exposed to everyone.

Ample interview research, dating back over eight decades, bears further witness to this proverb's instruction to weigh interviews lightly. To encapsulate it in a sentence, interviewers can do many things to improve the validity of an interview process, yet interviews tend to be very flawed measures of qualifications and character.[15] Using them, as we so often do, as the exclusive predictor of applicant fit and future performance is not a prudent move. They can remain the centerpiece of most staffing selection processes, but personal interviews should be heavily supplemented by the tools discussed above.

MEASURE APPLICANTS WISELY

The central advice of Proverbs on staffing is straightforward: sophisticate the process. Don't underestimate its importance. Don't underinvest in it. And don't do it informally.

In practice, and stated in the form of a managerial proverb, a sophisticated staffing process is one where we "measure twice, hire once." The first of these measures entails the examination— the rigorous examination—of the essentials: knowledge, skills, work history, and other traditional criteria. Measure two, the gauging of applicant character, is often ignored but is equally important. When we measure these two areas, we are more likely to have a successful hire, one who is productive and reliable.

Remember, an applicant's character is as important as his or her credentials. In fact, the Book of Proverbs goes so far as to suggest that character be used as a litmus test in the hiring process. That's because when work needs to be done, great credentials and an effervescent personality can be undermined by things like dishonesty, a lackluster work ethic, or an insubordinate attitude. Although budget and time constraints may make measuring these traits cumbersome, institutionalizing character measures in the staffing process is one of the more strategic human resource investments that exists. It's a critical step in hiring, and ultimately in building a competitive workforce.

NOTES

1. This account is compiled from the following news items: "Gunmen Steal Chips from Computer Firm," *The Dallas Morning News*, 6 December 1994, 1A; "Five Charged in '94 Theft on Microchips," *The Dallas Morning News*, 22 March 1997, 37A; "Computer Chips Hot Item for Mob Linked Thieves," *The Cincinnati Post*, 11 April 1995, 2A.

2. Linda Micco, "Gang Members Infiltrate the Workplace," "HR News Online" (Washington, D. C.: Society for Human Resource Management, 1997); available on the Internet at www.shrm.org/hrnews/articles/0623cd4.htm.

3. "Gang Members Infiltrating Chicago Police Department," *Des Moines Register*, 8 October 1995, 3.

4. The case, known as Malorney v. B & L Motor Freight, Inc., 496 N.E.2d 1086 (Ill. App. 1986), is cited in Mark Rothstein and Lance Liebman, *Employment Law*, 3rd ed. (Westbury, N.Y: Foundation Press, 1994), 143–46.

5. The United States Supreme Court settled this issue in NLRB v. Town and Country Electric, Inc. 116 S.Ct. 450

(1995).

6. "Many Falsify Credentials, Qualifications," *Atlanta Journal-Constitution*, 11 May 1992, B5.

7. Christopher J. Bachler, "Résumé Fraud: Lies, Omissions, and Exaggerations," *Personnel Journal*, 74, no. 6 (June 1995): 50–60.

8. See, for example, Sidney Gael, ed., vols. 1 and 2, *The Job Analysis Handbook for Business, Industry, and Government* (New York: John Wiley & Sons, 1988).

9. "Reference Checking Leaves Employers in the Dark, SHRM Says," Press Release detailing the survey results, Society for Human Resource Management, 26 June 1995; available on Internet at www.shrm.org.

10. In light of the importance of character references, though, one can avoid some of the dilemma by keeping the recruiting process largely in-house. Both internal promotion (see Principle 12) and employee referral systems are cost-effective recruitment strategies that result in placing individuals of more predictable ability and repute.

11. See, for example, H. John Bernardin and Donna K. Cooke, "Validity of an Honesty Test in Predicting Theft Among Convenience Store Employees," *Academy of Management Journal*, 36, no. 5 (1993): 1097–1108. See also Paul R. Sackett and James S. Wanek, "New Developments in the Use of Measures of Honesty, Integrity, Conscientiousness, Dependability, Trustworthiness, and Reliability for Personnel Selection," *Personnel Psychology* 49, no. 4 (1996): 787–829.

12. See, for example, Joyce Hogan and Robert Hogan, "How to Measure Employee Reliability," *Journal of Applied Psychology*, 74, no. 2 (1989): 273–79.

13. Regarding integrity tests, see Deniz S. Ones, Chockalingham Viswesvaran, and Frank L. Schmidt, "Comprehensive Meta-Analysis of Integrity Test Validities: Findings and Implications for Personnel Selection and Theories of Job Performance," *Journal of Applied Psychology*, 78, no. 4 (1993): 679–703.

   For evidence on the validity of personality tests, see Laetta M. Hough et al., "Criterion-Related Validities of Personality Constructs and the Effect of Response Distortions on those Validities," *Journal of Applied Psychology*, 75, no. 5 (1990): 581–95. See also Deniz S. Ones, Chockalingham Viswesvaran, and Angelika D. Reiss, "Role of Social Desirability in Personality Testing for Personnel Selection: The Red Herring," *Journal of Applied Psychology*, 81, no. 6 (1996): 660–679.

14. See, for example, George T. Milkovich and John W. Boudreau, *Human Resource Management,* 8th ed. (Chicago: Irwin, 1997), 256.

15. Among the more recent literature reviews summarizing the interview research are Richard D. Arvey and Michael A. Campion, "The Employment Interview: A Summary and Review of Recent Research," *Personnel Psychology,* 35, no. 2 (1982): 281–322; and Michael M. Harris, "Reconsidering the Employment Interview: A Review of Recent Literature and Suggestions for Future Research," *Personnel Psychology,* 42, no. 4 (1989): 691–720.

OFFER APPLICANTS A REALISTIC JOB PREVIEW

How's this for the ideal job? Sun, surf, tennis, golf, scuba diving, great food provided free of charge, and you can mingle with carefree people day after day. You get health insurance, full coverage of your living expenses, and at the end of the month, you even get a few hundred bucks for your bank account. These are among the many benefits of working at Club Med.

Sounds like the kind of place where people would be beating down the door to get a job. And historically this has been true. Most years, Club Med has so many applicants that only about one in twenty is offered a position. Paradoxically, though, despite the working environment and competition for employment, new hires at Club Med—a vacation mecca with locations around the world—have turned over at annual rates of up to 50 percent!

This is expensive. Not only does it generate enormous employee-replacement costs, but the exodus of new employees also disrupts guests' vacations. Wind-surfing instructors and tennis pros disappearing in midweek is simply intolerable in a business that lives and dies by customer satisfaction and word-of-mouth advertising.

So management did some research into the turnover problem and identified as a central culprit the patently unrealistic job expectations of new hires. Many of these folks (most of whom were in their twenties) envisioned being paid to take a perpetual vacation. However, this mirage evaporated in the island heat the moment they arrived at their paradise-like place of employment. Workdays at the Club spanned fifteen to sixteen hours and, regardless of one's exhaustion or mood, a Club Med employee was expected to continually effervesce with enthusiasm. Interaction with the eclectic assembly of guests, a chief selling point during the interview, turned out to be both incessant and vapid. Parting comments of quitting employees summarized the determinative concerns: "All we ever do is work and sleep," "My mind was going to waste down here on Gilligan's Island," and "How many times can you tell a [guest] to sign up for snorkeling before you go bonkers?" To the new hire, the shocking reality was that employment at Club Med seemed more like work than fun![1]

Because there are negative dimensions to every job, managers with staffing responsibilities confront the age-old question of how much to reveal to job applicants about a vacant position. Is it prudent, for example, to explicitly inform a prospective bank teller that she'll be standing on her feet all day, be dealing with irate customers on a regular basis, and be unable to avoid some weekend work? If we present these facts as a matter of policy, isn't there a significant risk of scaring away good candidates or having them demand more money to compensate for the arduous aspects of the job? However, if we do not present a realistic preview of what the job entails, do we not leave applicants to paint their own speculative and perhaps faulty picture of life in our organization, which could lead to costly ramifications like those experienced by Club Med?

From a business perspective, there are clearly advantages and disadvantages to both approaches. And, as we will see, there is a wealth of empirical literature that details the pros and cons. However, divine wisdom on offering realistic job previews dates back much further.

A PROVERB ON SETTING
JOB EXPECTATIONS

The key proverb on setting job expectations for prospective employees makes clear that truthfulness should be paramount:

The Lord detests lying lips, but he delights in men who are truthful.
(Proverbs 12:22)

This familiar teaching about honesty is relatively plain. Here we have the fundamental and quite intuitive truth: Honesty is an elemental virtue. That truth transcends almost every system of ethics, whether religious or philosophical.

What distinguishes the Judeo-Christian construction of this doctrine, though, is its insight into God's vehemence about honesty. We are not told to be honest because lying can harm others. Nor are we to be honest because it's the nice thing to do. Rather, the mandate is far more compelling: We must be honest because when we're not, *the Lord detests it*. Our dishonesty is an *abomination* to Him, as 12:22 is translated in the King James Version.

This is not a casual point. The Bible does not treat lightly the concept of God detesting something. In fact, "an abomination to God" is reserved for the most egregious offenses; for example, worshiping idols (Deuteronomy 7:25–26), pride and haughtiness (Proverbs 6:16–17), murder of the innocent (Proverbs 6:17), eagerness to do evil (Proverbs 6:18), creation of conflict among believers (Proverbs 6:19), the practices of homosexuality (Leviticus 18:22), cross-dressing (Deuteronomy 22:5), and buying a prostitute (Deuteronomy 23:18).

And dishonesty. For generations, some in Israel thought that dishonesty was no big deal, so God's inspired messengers like Solomon and Zechariah (Zechariah 8:16–17) underscored that it is indeed a big deal by including the sin amongst this distinguished list of what God hates. A few thousand years later, like the Israelites of Solomon's day, we again live in a culture that brushes off dishonesty as a tepid transgression ("After all, everybody does it!") and completely rationalizes it ("They're not paying me enough, so why not have lunch on the company credit card?"). But the Christian is called to resist conforming to that culture. Our challenge, as always, is to see our behavior not through the eyes of our postmodern society's standards, not through the eyes of our corporate culture, and not through the eyes of our boss. We must elevate our behavior, as we view our actions through the eyes of God. Dishonesty and deception are wholly unacceptable to God. They separate us from Him.

Applying this teaching to our interview setting, then, it would seem that not only is it sinful to lie about the nature or duties of a job we are attempting to fill, but, beyond this explicit dishonesty, it would also be improper to remain silent about the downside of a job. We are asking an applicant to give up his or her present job to take one with us. Or we may be inviting a presently unemployed individual to forego other opportunities to sign on at our firm. Moreover, through what we tell and do not tell an applicant, we are setting expectations for the job and thereby influencing future job satisfaction.

These are not innocuous things. Our unwillingness or neglect to disclose the negative dimensions of a position is a form of misrepresentation. Scripture invites us to see this all-too-customary practice for what it is, to see it as God does, and to be candid with job applicants.

RESEARCH ON REALISTIC JOB PREVIEWS

For decades, researchers in business management have sung the praises of realistic job preview, known as RJP. [2] As the term implies, this is a realistic communication to an applicant of both the positive and negative aspects of a job. The theory underlying RJP is that an organization can minimize turnover by encouraging those applicants who would most likely quit as a result of a poor fit with the organization to excuse themselves from the hiring process before any offer is made. In doing so, they allow an organization to reduce its employee-replacement costs (i.e., recruitment, selection, orientation, training). Moreover, since those who have more realistic expectations about a job will be less surprised by its dissatisfying facets, they should be more satisfied with the new job and thus become more productive than if they had not been given a realistic preview.

The findings of this mature line of research generally comport with the theory. Indeed, RJP lowers initial expectations about a job and consequently increases employee retention. This is especially true for more complex jobs where an applicant would be less likely to anticipate all that the job entails. The cost savings vary inversely with the severity of an organization's turnover problem: To date, our best estimates forecast a 12 percent employee-replacement cost savings for an organization with a 50 percent turnover rate, and a 6 percent cost savings for an organization with an 80 percent turnover rate. Productivity effects remain a bit more of an open question, with research more cautiously predicting productivity gains from RJP only during the first year of a new employee's tenure.

So in light of these empirical conclusions, is it always a good idea, from a business perspective, to offer applicants an RJP? Does it always pay to be honest and forthright with prospective employees? The management literature resoundingly says no. Where an applicant pool is small or does not contain many qualified individuals, furnishing negative information about a job can, in fact, lead to the position going unfilled—often a worse consequence than having it filled by a dissatisfied new employee who will eventually quit. Accordingly, the recommendation of mainstream management scholars would be to use RJP only where one has a rich pool of fully qualified people from which to choose.

Herein lies the tension with Scripture, of course. No such caveat exists in words like: "The Lord detests lying lips, but he delights in men who are truthful." It's unequivocal. Additionally, Proverbs speaks to this very point of deception for profit's sake in 21:6 : "A fortune made by a lying tongue is a fleeting vapor and a deadly snare." It would seem, therefore, that, independent of profit-maximization rationales, Scripture asks us to use RJP—to be truthful with applicants—regardless of the size or quality of the candidate pool.

In recognition of this implicit charge to offer a realistic job preview, what follows here are some suggestions from the research on designing and implementing such a system.

OPTIONS FOR DESIGNING
AN RJP SYSTEM

It is important to recognize at the outset that there is no one right way to do this. Rather, a better way to think about the design of an RJP system is to see it as providing several choices that must complement an organization's staffing procedures. The company needs to make choices in at least four major areas. [3]

First, one must decide *whether the information presented to the job applicant will be primarily "descriptive" or "judgmental."* The descriptive approach simply imparts objective information about the job: time to promotion, hours expected, likelihood of salary increases, etc. It allows the individual applicant to discern for him or herself the good, the bad, and the ugly in a job. By contrast, the "judgmental" approach concentrates more on those things that current employees find most satisfying and dissatisfying. This option entails collecting data from employees about how they feel about the job (e.g., "Employees dislike how long it takes to get promoted") and then presenting these conclusions to applicants. It tends to be most useful for younger, more naive applicants who may be unable to draw proper inferences about the job from descriptive information. Of course, the descriptive and judgmental approaches are not mutually exclusive, but time or cost limitations often compel one to choose between the two.

A second decision involves *the extent of information presented to the applicant.* The company hiring representative can seek to comprehensively cover the positive and negative qualities inherent in a job or instead choose to focus on the most important elements, those "satisfiers" and "dissatisfiers" for employees. In practice, the choice is one of breadth versus depth, and each has obvious advantages. To best effect the self-selection process, though, many organizations elect the latter option; in that way the most crucial job information does not get lost amidst the sea of facts to which the applicant is exposed.

A third decision is *the selection of a medium for RJP.* Most organizations use either a brochure or a video to communicate the satisfiers and dissatisfiers of their work environment. The brochure approach is cheaper, easier to modify when jobs change, and can be reread by applicants. With a video (shown as part of the interview), one can be more certain that the applicant has actually seen the RJP. In the few comparative tests that exist, researchers have concluded that video tends to produce moderately superior results to brochures, especially if the video presents real employees describing the job in their own words. One can also, of course, give the RJP inperson during a personal interview. And in fact, there is some empirical evidence indicating that in-person RJP may be superior to both written and video formats since applicants perceive a greater sense of organizational honesty flowing from in-person statements.[4]

A fourth decision is *whether to offer the RJP early or late in the employee selection process.* Doing it later has the advantage of being cheaper, since fewer candidates remain in the pool. However, an important disadvantage of late RJP must be weighed: An applicant will sometimes build an artificial commitment to an organization if he or she surmounts the first couple hurdles. Offering an RJP at this late stage may therefore be less effective, since poorly fitting individuals may not self-select out of the process.

AVOIDING DECEPTION AND DISHONESTY

The temptations of deception and dishonesty are as powerful and as prevalent as any other temptation in the workplace. We can deceitfully advance our organizational objectives by over-selling the quality of our product or service, by neglecting to reveal hidden costs to customers, by "cooking the books" in accounting, by finessing the details of a prospectus to better raise capital, by duping the IRS—the list is endless. Something we seldom think about, but something that surely resides on this inventory of deceptive practices, is neglecting to be forthright with job applicants about what they're getting themselves into.

As noted, realistic job preview is a management tool that in some but not all cases adds value from a bottom-line perspective. However, those managing in Christ's image should not practice RJP merely for that positive organizational benefit. God's will must predominate, and Scripture is our consummate compass. Honesty and integrity are the Scripture's call upon us.

Thus, in those instances where we will likely incur some cost with little return for being completely honest with job candidates, we should not allow that cost to cloud the inherent virtue in this policy: God "delights in men who are truthful."

NOTES

1. For more information on this case, see "Club Med," Harvard Business School case 9-687-047 (1986); available from HBS Press, Cambridge, Massachusetts, 800-545-7685.
2. Research conclusions for this section have been derived from the following sources: Glenn M. McEvoy and Wayne F. Cascio, "Strategies for Reducing Employee

Turnover: A Meta Analysis," *Journal of Applied Psychology*, 70, no. 2 (1985): 342–53; Steven L. Premack and John P. Wanous, "A Meta-Analysis of Realistic Job Preview Experiments," *Journal of Applied Psychology*, 70, no. 4 (1985): 706–19; Roger A. Dean and John P. Wanous, "The Effects of Realistic Job Previews On Hiring Bank Tellers," *Journal of Applied Psychology*, 69, no. 1 (1984): 61–68; and Bruce M. Meglino, Elizabeth C. Ravlin, and Angelo S. DeNisi, "When Does It Hurt to Tell the Truth? The Effect of Realistic Job Previews On Employee Recruiting," *Public Personnel Management*, 26, no. 3 (Fall 1997): 413–23.

3. Some of what follows in this section is derived from John P. Wanous, "Installing a Realistic Job Preview: Ten Tough Choices," *Personnel Psychology*, 42, no. 1 (1989): 117–34.

4. See Stephen M. Colarelli, "Methods of Communication and Mediating Processes in Realistic Job Previews," *Journal of Applied Psychology*, 69, no. 4 (1984): 633–42.

SELECT CAREFULLY
YOUR
MANAGEMENT TEAM

Dear Citizens. I have signed a decree on dismissing the government. [Prime Minister] Viktor Stepanovich Chernomyrdin is also being dismissed. It's never easy to part with old colleagues. We worked together for more than five years."

On March 23, 1998, President Boris Yeltsin appeared on Russian television to announce the firing of his entire cabinet. He explained the shake-up this way:

> The current cabinet team solved a series of tasks that it faced but unfortunately could not cope with a number of key questions. Yes, we achieved certain changes in the economy, but we are still lagging far behind in the social sphere. People do not feel the changes for the better. . . .
>
> In a word, the country needs a new team, ca-

pable of achieving real, discernible results. I think the members of the cabinet must concentrate more on solving economic and social issues, and be less involved with politics. . . .

I am very much counting on your support and understanding, dear Russians. In the near future our country will have a new civil government. Thank you for your attention.[1]

Yeltsin justified the move as an attempt to tap new blood and fresh ideas where lethargy and politics had for far too long prevailed. Economic and social reforms were stagnant, warranting extreme remedial action, the president claimed. Soon thereafter, though, for reasons that were not entirely clear, Yeltsin relented, deciding to retain most of the cabinet. But in doing so, he issued a foreboding statement regarding his expectations for those in top government positions.

"We must create an environment in which everyone knows and feels that a failure to fulfill orders means death," Yeltsin avowed with a stern frown. "You will have to immediately submit your resignation."[2]

Even to this day, reasons for the 1998 shake-up in the Russian top brass remain obscure. But regardless of the true impetus for this bizarre sequence of events, Yeltsin's stated motivation for cleaning house as well as his later unbridled threat should resonate with most who occupy the top spot in an organization. Whether one is heading a large company, a small business, a church, or a superpower, proper implementation of the top person's vision requires full support of that vision from the organization's upper echelon. Significant variance in agendas and philosophies at the top of any organization can lead to power struggles, suffocate synergy among units, slow response to changing markets and customer demands, and, ultimately, compromise organizational effectiveness. The staffing implication, therefore, is that *one must be highly discriminating in selecting one's inner circle of managers*.

Additionally, there is a personal reason for Christians who lead organizations to encircle themselves with like-minded personnel: The people around us often shape our attitudes and our behaviors. Over time, if the vista of those near to us sharply contrasts with our own, these individuals may not only fail to implement our vision, they may actually begin to *transform* that vision. That is, they may change our conception of both the organizational mission and the role of its leader. They may subtly, even unintentionally, shepherd us toward a secularized business mindset. Such a transformation would be especially problematic for a Christian whose original intent is to run his or her organization for the glory of God (Principle 1).

Even if the chief executive can ignore or dissuade senior managers who threaten to alter the corporate vision, he may spend much time and mental energy clarifying and vetoing their suggestions. He may feel frustration and fatigue facing his resisters at various junctures. Although he does not want "yes men" surrounding him, the leader needs the top managers to have a similar vision and value system.

So both for organizational performance reasons and for personal reasons, the Christian leader must be cautious about those with whom he or she consorts. This is a fundamental principle of association and, interestingly, one that flows from the Book of Proverbs.

PROVERBS ON CHOOSING ASSOCIATES WISELY

Proverbs offers several nuggets of advice on the positive and negative consequences of association. Among the most precise is this one:

He who walks with the wise grows wise, but a companion of fools suffers harm.
(Proverbs 13:20)

Many have experienced the truth of this proverb firsthand. Anyone who has spent a significant amount of time fraternizing with discerning, God-fearing individuals may have soon found him or herself thinking and speaking like these people, adopting their critical-thinking skills, procuring their arguments, and embracing their worldview. Attributes of the "wise" can to some degree become our attributes simply by prolonged exposure to them.

Similarly, as indicated by the second half of the proverb, this principle of gradual metamorphosis can work against us when we choose friends inattentively. Associating with "fools," we are told, leads to "harm."

However, the adverse consequence here is not quite as tepid as the English translation makes it appear. Recall from the introductory chapter of this book that the "fool" in Proverbs is not just one who is foolish, but one who does not respect God and who is morally suspect. In this light, Proverbs 13:20 is alerting us to the very serious risk inherent in close association with those who have rejected God's narrow road in favor of the world's superhighway: These people encourage us to carpool with them.

And as we delve more deeply into the Book of Proverbs, we find that the admonition is not an isolated one. God warns us repeatedly about being pulled from Him by those who do not trust in His ways (e.g., Proverbs 10:17; 12:26; 14:7). Lest this is too vague, chapter 22 offers us a specific example of a character trait that can be contagious:

> *Do not make friends with a hot-tempered man, do not associate with one easily angered, or you may learn his ways and get yourself ensnared.*
> (Proverbs 22:24–25)

No abstraction here. The proverb speaks plainly to another common experience, one that is particularly germane to the workplace where complaining, gossiping, revenge, and outright hostility so often thrive. Who has not worked with an individual that fits the description of verse 24? And who among us, having worked closely with such an individual, has not "learned his ways" and begun to act at least a little like this person? We can become infected, complaining and gossiping along with the individual, responding as he vengefully responds, rather than as Christ would respond. The causal relationship between associating with one easily angered and becoming easily angered is direct and virulent, so the Christian must be evervigilant here.

The consistent message through all of these verses, then, is that because of the tendency to become like those around us, "a righteous man is [to be] cautious in friendship" (Proverbs 12:26a). The theme is also expressed in the New Testament, as Paul told the Corinthians that foolishness can beget foolishness ("Bad company corrupts good character," according to 1 Corinthians 15:33) and the Colossians that wisdom can beget wisdom ("Teach and admonish one another with all wisdom," according to Colossians 3:16). Therefore, Christians in leadership positions, whether CEOs or budding entrepreneurs, pastors or politicians, would be well-served by heeding the scriptural advice to actively discriminate when selecting close associates.

STAFFING TOP SPOTS
AT AMERICAN GREETINGS

Two problems appear to flow from this staffing principle.

First, does the principle require that to be in top management one must attend the "right" church? Hardly. In fact, besides violating antidiscrimination laws, a "Christian-only" hiring and promotion policy is not a biblical mandate. Instead, the solution that comports with God and man's laws and makes good business sense is to use the following criterion: Fill top spots with people who wholly embrace the company's ethics and operating principles. They need not be Christian, but they must have an unwavering commitment to the company's vision and strategic direction. On this standard, we should not compromise.

This leads us to the second problem: implementation. How does one identify individuals who both fit this ethical mold and have the skills and knowledge necessary to succeed at the executive level? And how does one do so efficiently? The system used by American Greeting Corporation, a greeting card manufacturer based in Cleveland, offers a useful case study on how to efficiently staff top spots with loyal, proficient individuals.[3]

When high-level positions at American Greetings become vacant, there is no crisis, no extended search, and little lost productivity. Moreover, the search typically culminates in the selection of an exceedingly competent manager who understands the intricacies of the organization, who commands the requisite skills to succeed, and who will be a long-term player. This happens because the new corner office occupant is the product of a deliberate process that generates a rich, internal "talent pool."

A team of four persons—the CEO, the president, the vice-president of human resources, and the director of development—comprise what

American Greetings calls its "executive development committee." The group is charged with
identifying high-potential in-house candidates
for the company's top three levels of management
(about 125 senior vice-presidents, vice-presidents, and executive directors). As members of
the executive development committee nominate
candidates with strong leadership potential, the
committee scrutinizes each nominee's competencies and compares these competencies with the
attributes necessary to perform in the top positions. Through this comparison, the committee
ascertains "competency gaps" for each nominee
and then seeks to bridge those gaps by assigning
the promising employee "developmental tasks"
that specifically target the shortcoming. Upon
completion of the developmental task, the manager presents his or her results to the executive
development committee, thus permitting the
committee to further evaluate the manager's potential.

This logical, somewhat mechanical system of
professional development both improves the individual's performance in his or her current position and gives American Greetings a large pool of
potential successors for each top management
position that becomes vacant. The approach,
since it offers so much flexibility in staffing,
therefore remains far superior to the more commonplace practices of maintaining a list of potential successors for each position, or staffing
upper-level positions on an ad hoc basis.

Moreover, the system provides the committee
a significant amount of information on a job as-
pirant's character, values, and willingness to com-

ply with the corporate vision—intangibles that are often difficult to measure in an external candidate. Lastly, and perhaps most importantly, the internal candidate who has been groomed in this manner has been socialized and inculcated into the corporate vision that he or she is expected to implement.

There is an interesting parallel here with the Gospel. Although neither the Gospel nor Christianity is the catalyst at American Greetings, staff development and the internal recruitment system are similar to the approach that Christ Himself used with His team of apostles. Each was thoroughly trained in the vision of the Master, each had competency gaps that were filled through such "developmental tasks" as being sent out to evangelize, and each was later commissioned to succeed Him after His death. A further parallel is in the "promotion" of Peter to the status of "rock." Christ had essentially shaped a "talent pool" and from it emerged one man who, because he saw as the Leader saw, was elevated above the rest.

As for the others, though, they too (with only one casualty, which Jesus Himself foresaw) ultimately excelled in their roles because of their training and their exposure to Jesus. Which of course brings us back full circle to Proverbs 13:20. The apostles became wise because they walked with the epitome of wisdom. And in doing so, they became more competent to carry forward the mission of their CEO. This system may be operationalized in many organizations today, but indeed, two thousand years ago witnessed succession planning at its very best.

DISCRIMINATE WHEN
SELECTING MANAGERS

Every leader must carefully select the management team. In fact, discriminate when selecting your management team.

The word *discriminate* has taken on an offensive connotation in the workplace, but, in point of fact, this is *precisely* what the Christian leader is called to do when assembling his or her management team. We are admonished by Scripture to be highly selective and to screen out those whose vision is inconsistent with our values and the direction we have set for our organization.

As noted earlier, this does not necessarily mean that one promotes only Christians to such positions (in fact, outside of religious organizations, this practice would be illegal). Nor does it necessarily mean that one need impetuously fire the current team in an effort to revitalize the organization.

It would seem to imply, however, at least two things. First, *one should make a priority of preparing people to serve in this capacity*. This takes time, and it takes money. But it is surely a worthwhile investment. Second, when the time comes to make a selection, *one should resist any impulse to staff these positions solely by tangible credentials like education and experience*. Beyond these attributes, it is one's intangible wisdom qualities, according to Proverbs, that truly qualify one to manage alongside the Christian leader.

NOTES

1. Reuters News Service, "Text of Boris Yeltsin's Televised Statement," *The New York Times,* 24 March 1998, A8.

2. Associated Press, "Yeltsin Will Keep Some Key Ministers," *The Cincinnati Post,* 24 March 1998, A2.
3. Information on American Greetings comes from Shari
   Caudron, "Plan Today for an Unexpected Tomorrow,"
   Personnel Journal, 75, no. 9 (September 1996), 40–45.

INVEST
IN
EMPLOYEE
TRAINING

On the evening of August 30, 1980, Officers Burbine and Stawecki of the Farmington (New Hampshire) Police Department were on routine patrol monitoring Route 11. Burbine, an experienced officer, was assigned to give on-the-job training to his partner who had joined the force only two weeks earlier. Prior to his assignment with Burbine, Stawecki had received no formal instruction in police work.

After the pair observed a truck wandering across the center line, they followed it down the road and into the parking lot of Luneau's Restaurant. As the officers approached the vehicle, the driver, Carroll Cutter, exited and was told by Stawecki to put his hands on the truck. Carroll resisted, demanding that he first be told what he had done. As Stawecki repeated the order, Carroll reached for something in his pants pocket. Stawecki immediately grabbed Carroll's hand and pushed him to the ground. The rookie officer then got on top of Carroll and handcuffed him while Burbine looked on and occasionally assisted.

En route to the police station, Carroll told the officers on at least two occasions that the handcuffs were too tight; however, in part because Carroll was doing so much kicking and screaming, the request for looser handcuffs went unheeded.

This sequence of events precipitated a lawsuit where Carroll presented evidence that the handcuff pressure had caused permanent damage to the radial nerve in his left wrist, thereby making him unfit for his job as a logger and trucker. Apparently, Officer Stawecki had failed to properly "double lock" the cuffs, causing them to continue tightening from the time of application in the restaurant parking lot to the time of their removal at the police station. Based on this evidence, the jury found Stawecki's employer, the Town of Farmington, guilty of something called "negligent training," a novel cause of action at the time. Concluding that the employer had failed to take reasonable care in preparing Stawecki for duty, they awarded Carroll $55,000 in damages. The town lost its appeals all the way to the New Hampshire Supreme Court.[1]

In an increasing number of jurisdictions, employers are being held legally liable for the failure to train their employees. This is in part because judges and juries perceive a connection between employee training and such outcomes as safety, competence, and quality, and then conclude that employers should be investing in such training.

Many in management perceive these connections as well, evidenced by the fact that innumerable organizations of every size collectively invest billions each year in employee training. However, the investment exists not so much to insulate employers from legal liability as it does because employers believe it's good business. Once seen as a frill, employee training is now considered by many a source of competitive advantage.

This is especially true in light of twenty-first century work systems that rely heavily on employee skill, flexibility, and initiative. Those on the frontlines of production or service are increasingly called upon to identify and resolve problems, to initiate changes in the work methods, and to take responsibility for quality.

It's no surprise, then, that there is perhaps more information available on employee training than on any other employee-management function. Indeed, many of the ideas may at first glance wreak of trendiness (especially when one sees buzzwords like *knowledge management, intellectual capital,* and *learning organizations*), but from the reaction of top management, the movement is likely here to stay. Approximately one-fifth of Fortune 500 firms have created the position of "chief knowledge officer" (or some comparable title), often reporting directly to the CEO.[2]

A PROVERB ON EMPLOYEE TRAINING

Our ultimate CEO may have a similar concern for employee training, as expressed through one of His own chief knowledge officers in the Book of Proverbs.

Scripture counsels us on the importance of putting first things first. Especially noteworthy is the following proverb:

*Finish your outdoor work and get
your fields ready; after that,
build your house.*
(Proverbs 24:27)

Because ancient Israel was an agricultural society, many proverbs employ farming imagery. For the same reason, Christ used agricultural settings for many of His parables, including the workers in the vineyard (Matthew 20:1–16), the sower and the soils (Matthew 13:1–23; Mark 4:1–20; Luke 8:1–15), and the prodigal son (Luke 15:11–32). Agriculture was the original community's frame of reference, so using it as a backdrop was a powerful way to teach timeless truths.

One need not be a farmer to understand Proverbs 24:27, though. From a literal perspective, if one who has purchased land cultivates the field before building the house, then the crops will be growing while one is engaged in another project. It's more efficient to operate this way. It's strategic. Moreover, it culminates in a higher-quality house since, as the crops mature, their yield helps one buy more and better construction materials.

First Things First

The proverb also suggests that the principle of "first things first" applies generally to any human enterprise. The term "build your house" is often used as a scriptural metaphor for undertaking an important endeavor. In Matthew's gospel, for instance, Christ instructs us to be wise and build our spiritual house upon His rock (Matthew 7:24–27). Similar use of the phrase comes from the author of Hebrews who likens Jesus to a house builder, when he writes that Jesus is greater than Moses "just as the builder of a house has greater honor than the house itself" (Hebrews 3:3). Many more examples of this kind exist (e.g., Psalms 127:1; Proverbs 24:3–4).

In Proverbs 24:27, God's counsel is that before we commence any significant venture, we should lay a firm foundation for its success. This instruction has myriad applications. For instance, in evangelism, one should learn what is in Scripture before one attempts to communicate what God's Word says. In rearing children, a parent's own spiritual house must be in order before he or she can consistently model right living for the children. Likewise, in any attempt to manage from a scriptural perspective, a business leader should begin by adopting the appropriate set of attitudes (including the four attitudes in part 1). First things should come first.

With specific regard to staffing, one might interpret the proverb as advising that a new hire is like a "field" that one has just purchased, and the work this individual is hired to perform is the "house" to be built. Thus, step one would be to cultivate the field: to train the new hire.

But this is not always natural for us to do. Upon hiring an employee, a manager may be anxious to immediately get the house built—to immerse this new hire in the tasks to be performed —so as to recoup the salary and benefits invested in this person. In other words, it is tempting to neglect the field cultivation in favor of letting it (the employee) grow on its own. Besides, we reason, the field already has some crops. We wouldn't have purchased it otherwise.

A Preliminary Investment in Training

Proverbs suggests that this type of thinking may be impetuous. Rather than expect new employees to immediately bear fruit, it is often better to take the strategic road of investing time and money in one's people. There are indeed costs up front, but the long-term payout may be much greater.

Moreover, the logical extension of this reasoning would encourage the continuation of this training investment beyond the new hire stage. Since "house-building" in a business context is an ongoing process, so too should be the preparation of one's fields. Just as farmers cultivate regularly, so too should the manager of employees develop the employees' careers (as described later in Principle 12).

Put first things first, God's wisdom counsels us. For both new hires and veteran employees, make it standard operating procedure to invest in training.

COSTS AND RETURN ON INVESTMENT

For decades, the scholarly community has vigorously examined employee training issues. Training researchers have made great strides in empirically identifying some of the elements of effective training programs. The four that appear to be most widely cited are: (1) a top management willingness to make training part of the corporate culture, (2) a close connection between training objectives and business strategy, (3) a systematic approach to training that targets all levels on a continuous basis, and (4) a genuine commitment to invest the necessary resources for training to be done properly.[3]

Difficulties in Measuring the ROI

However, a critical question—and for many, *the* critical question—centers on a more threshold concern: *What's the return on investment?* Whether designing or purchasing employee training programs, whether training in-house, off-site, on or off the job, the decision to train typically carries with it a substantial price tag. Beyond the direct costs, there is also lost time, possible disruption to the work flow, and employee mistakes as workers creep up the learning curve in applying their training. So given the expense, it's only prudent to inquire about the payback.

Unfortunately, one of the great ironies in management research is that the scholarship reveals itself as wanting precisely where empirical guidance is needed most. This is a classic case in point: It is exceedingly difficult to accurately measure training's influence on productivity and quality outcomes. Because only a small minority of employees produce quantifiable output, most training outcomes are completely intangible or unobservable. Moreover, even where one can measure productivity and quality changes with some precision, these changes tend to be associated with so many variables that isolating the "training effect" is often impossible. Thus, the limitations of human research methodology have prevented academics from reaching any firm conclusions about training's return on investment (ROI).

These same deficiencies have blocked corporate efforts to evaluate their own training programs as well. Motorola, Inc., for instance, enthusiastically lauded for their innovative Motorola University and long cited as the standard in employee training, spends lavishly to develop its people. When asked about the return on this hefty outlay, though, an official from Motorola's training group says that "the company is notoriously poor at evaluating their $170 million investment in training."[4] They obviously believe there's a positive return, but both the measurement problems and the expense of evaluation remain insurmountable obstacles to ROI calculations.

Saturn Corporation is similarly hamstrung. Consistent with the proverbial model of cultivating the fields, new hires at Saturn receive between 300 and 600 hours of training their first year, and at least 92 hours per year thereafter. It is logical to expect that the training delivers returns on the assembly line, but in fact the actual return is indeterminate.[5]

Faith That Training Will Pay Dividends

What this seems to mean is that organizations that invest in employee training necessarily invest somewhat blindly. When one strips away all the fancy labels and glowing predictions of training's potential, most organizations' training investment is predicated on nothing more than an assumption that there's a connection between people and important work outcomes. The expenditure rests on an untested but intuitive faith that training pays dividends.

So what's the ROI for employee training? Does it pay, from a financial perspective, to invest in one's people? The answer, of course, will be a function of the specific program, the individuals involved, and other covariants cited above. But in general, the disappointing answer from academia and industry is "we don't really know."

CULTIVATING YOUR "FIELD" OF EMPLOYEES

It is on issues like these—issues where empirical research has failed to deliver satisfactory conclusions—that the value of God's Word shines that much more brightly. Proverbs offers sound counsel where human research and analysis cannot go.

In this particular case, God advises us to pursue an employee-management function that is easy to neglect. Regardless the size of one's team—one's "field" in scriptural language—its cultivation should be a top managerial priority. Training should precede the "house building" of getting work done.

Toward this end, Christian managers might consider tapping the voluminous resources in this area: computer web sites, trade journals, business magazines, and so on. There is no paucity of industry-specific information on how to implement employee training in a cost-effective, time-sensitive manner. Here, then, the central teaching of Proverbs 24:27 applies yet again: Before building one's training house, first cultivate and harvest the vast field of available ideas.

NOTES

1. *Carroll E. Cutter v. Town of Farmington*, 498 A.2d 316 (1985), New Hampshire Supreme Court.
2. Thomas A. Stewart, "Is This Job Really Necessary? On Balance, Yes," *Fortune*, 12 January 1998, 154–57.
3. See, for example, the extensive literature review in Wayne F. Cascio, *Applied Psychology in Human Resource Management* (Upper Saddle River, N. J.: Prentice-Hall, 1998), 259–78.
4. Jeffrey Pfeffer, "Seven Practices of Successful Organizations," *California Management Review*, 40, no. 2 (Winter 1998): 116.
5. Ibid., 114.

PART THREE

CULTIVATING
A
CULTURE
OF
COMMITMENT

BUILD ORGANIZATIONAL TRUST

Once upon a time there was a company called Eastern Airlines. It was always a reliable company, and it had hardworking employees, but eventually it found itself in some debt—$2.5 billion worth to be exact. So in 1983, Eastern's president, Frank Borman, went to his workers and their unions to ask for some assistance. "The company's going broke," he told them. "But I can save it if you take a big pay cut." The workers said no. They remembered that just a few short years ago, Mr. Borman fought hard to freeze their wages, so they didn't trust him very much.

Then the president threatened the workers: "Make these concessions or I *will* take Eastern into bankruptcy and none of you will have jobs!" The workers consented. They really had little choice. But in exchange for the concessions, the workers got to own 25 percent of the airline.

By 1986, the workers decided that owning a company that was losing $2 million a day was not such a good idea, so they demanded all of

their wage concessions back. Now it was Mr. Bor-
man's turn to say no. He did, however, give one
thousand of the workers a permanent vacation
and later sold the airline to another Frank, whose
last name was Lorenzo.

Mr. Lorenzo and the unions did not work well
together either. In 1988, when he too desperately
requested wage concessions, the workers voted by
a 99 percent majority to reject his proposal. The
next year, when the workers made contract demands, Mr. Lorenzo did the rejecting. He wouldn't
budge, so the workers went on strike.

The strike lasted about two years and in the
middle of it, Eastern's creditors went to court to
get Mr. Lorenzo fired and replaced by a trustee.
They got their trustee, but it was too late to stop
the bleeding. A few months later, the creditors demanded the liquidation of the airline, and in January of 1991, Eastern Airlines flew away forever.
And no one lived happily ever after.[1]

Eastern's civil war classically illustrates the destructive potential of labor-management distrust.
But it is one of an increasing number of examples. As we've moved toward a global marketplace and as business environments have become
more competitive, organizations are under con-
stant pressure to make rapid changes. Often,
these changes include asking employees to modify the terms of their employment: to accept more
job responsibilities, to work more hours, to be
paid for performance, to retrain, to work in
teams, and so on. Perhaps this trend explains
why a majority of employees now perceive that
their employer has breached some aspect of the
employment agreement.[2]

"Organizational trust," defined in one management journal as a willingness of an employee and employer to be vulnerable to one another and to take risks for one another,[3] is fast becoming a critical determinant of organizational success. From a top-management perspective, it is a precursor to employee acceptance of strategic initiatives, a sine qua non for the flexibility demanded by a dynamic business environment. From the perspective of lower-level managers, shrinking resources and staff make synergy between boss and subordinate more important than ever; but without trust, this synergy is limited.

At every level in every organization, though, the starting point for building this invisible asset is always the same: *A leader cultivates trust by first being trustworthy.* This principle we learn from Proverbs.

A PROVERB ON BUILDING TRUST

What Solomon Learned

Solomon, Israel's third king (after Saul and David), knew much about leadership. He stood at the nation's helm during a time of unprecedented prosperity. Among his three-thousand-plus proverbs, he wrote:

> *Love and faithfulness keep a
> king safe; through love his
> throne is made secure.*
> (Proverbs 20:28)

The impetus for these words of Solomon was most likely Israel's experience with its first two earthly kings. Saul, as we read in the book of 1 Samuel, was originally extolled as a great warrior and consummate leader by the people of Israel. So they made this tall and handsome, yet humble man their king. (See 1 Samuel 10:20–27.) But later King Saul proved to be untrustworthy. He was unfaithful to God's instructions (e.g., 1 Samuel 13:9–13; 15:9–10) and displayed little love for the king's servants. For instance, in one colossal blunder of leadership, Saul demanded that, until his army defeated the Philistines in battle, none of them could eat (1 Samuel 14:24).

The insecurity of Saul really began to accelerate after young David slew the mighty Goliath, prompting all of Israel to hail David's military prowess as superior to that of the king (1 Samuel 18:7). In response, a jealous Saul tried to kill David, but only succeeded in chasing him into exile for a decade. Ultimately, this unloving, unfaithful king lost his throne by committing suicide (1 Samuel 31:4).

By contrast, the first half of King David's forty-year reign was characterized by fastidious adherence to God's Word and by the extension of loving acts toward his people (e.g., 2 Samuel 9). Indeed, no throne could have been more secure, as Israel during these years enjoyed a high standard of living, expanded its territory, and became the military powerhouse of the neighborhood.[4] No doubt, had pollsters been around, they would have reported David's job-approval ratings in the high 90s.

But then, like Saul, David breached the trust of

both God and man. We know the stories well. David adulterously cavorts with Bathsheba and then has her husband murdered. David's son Amnon rapes his half sister Tamar, and David does nothing about it. After stewing for two years over the injustice, David's son Absalom takes matters into his own hands, killing Amnon and seizing control of the kingdom from his father. As David's "love and faithfulness" unraveled, so did his throne.

Solomon's inspired reflection on these events undergirds the theory of effective, enduring leadership he chronicled in Proverbs 20:28. The attributes of love and faithfulness make a leader trustworthy, thereby engendering a reciprocal trust among his followers. Accordingly, the leader's influence is strengthened, "His throne is made secure."

Additional Perspective from Isaiah

But admittedly, for all of its truth, this "theory" seems a bit underdeveloped. The proverb offers only broad strokes, with little practical guidance about what it means for a leader to be loving and faithful. Fortunately, though, these exact terms are unpacked for us in a verse that is undeniably linked to Proverbs 20:28.

Isaiah 16:5, one of Isaiah's many prophesies of the coming Messiah, illuminates God's definitions of loving and faithful: "In love a throne will be established; in faithfulness a man will sit on it—one from the house of David—one who in judging seeks justice and speeds the cause of righteousness."

Here is the model, Isaiah wrote. This is what

the prototypical leader looks like. Anyone who aspires to godly leadership and who seeks a secure throne need look no further than the example of Christ. Love your followers as Christ loves His. Be as faithful to them as Christ is to you. In doing so, you will establish a fundamental bond of trust with your people.

So from a Christian perspective, this is the compelling leadership lesson of Proverbs 20:28: Emulate Christ for the people entrusted to you. That means that regardless of the cultural norms where you work, and independent of how anyone treats you, model Christ's love and faithfulness in the management of your subordinates. Herein lies the foundation for building trust and insuring long-term leadership success.

FINDINGS ON ORGANIZATIONAL TRUST

A "Psychological Contract" Between Employer and Employee

Since the 1950s, researchers have examined how this teaching operates in the work world, formally inquiring into how organizational trust is created, how it's undermined, and how it's linked to organizational effectiveness.[5] They have concluded that employees view their relationship with an employer in terms of reciprocal obligations. Academics have called this the "psychological contract" of the workplace,[6] but in plain English, it simply means that employees perceive that there is an unwritten bargain in place between employer and employee. The employee's end of the bargain is to do a decent job and to function within the established rules of conduct for the workplace. In exchange for this, the employee believes the employer has obligations in the areas of pay, promotion, job security, work assignments, hours required, and so on.

Much organizational trust research focuses on what happens when these employee expectations are not met—when, from the employee's perspective, the employer has breached the psychological contract. In the context of proverbial wisdom, the researchers have primarily asked: "What happens when an employee thinks that the employer has done something contrary to the instruction of Proverbs 20:28?"; that is, when the boss does not show love and faithfulness.

As might be anticipated, the consequences can be pretty grave. When an employee perceives a breach of trust on the part of management—for instance, when he does not get an expected pay raise with the annual review—the research predicts lower performance from this person and reduced "citizenship" behaviors, such as concern about the success of the organization, department, or work group; perceived obligations toward the employer; and courtesy toward those in management. In addition, researchers found a higher propensity for such employees to leave the company, contributing to higher turnover rates.[7]

These studies further indicate that this employee will be less trusting of management in the future and, most importantly, *this employee will be more likely to perceive almost any future change in the status quo as a breach of management's end of the bargain.* That is, he may be quick to cry foul at even the most innocuous managerial decisions. And in the larger picture, when a mind-set of low trust permeates an organization's workforce, major consequences exist for organizational performance.

For example, let's say that a company has purchased some new computerized machinery to expedite the manufacturing process. Management is now explaining the rationale for the new system to the employees who will use it, pitching the technology as necessary to keep production costs down so the company can remain competitive. They're basically asking for workers to accept an initiative that will require their retraining, the developing of new skills, and the unease of setting aside their old way of doing things for a new way. What will be the employees' response?

In a Work Culture of Low Trust

If this is a work culture of low trust, both the research and common sense predict vehement resistance. Employees will respond with comments like: "Why should I care about competition and costs? That's your problem, not mine." "'New technology' is just management code for 'work faster!'" "How many jobs is this going to cost us?" Some may query sarcastically, "What was the phone number of that labor union?" And, of course, many may ask, "What kind of raise comes with this?"

Self-serving attitudes and behaviors are common manifestations of a distrusting culture. They will stunt an organization's growth and effectiveness. Or they may yield even worse outcomes: As with Eastern Airlines, such attitudes can preclude the flexibility that is necessary for survival.

However, to the same extent that low trust pro-

duces a competitive disadvantage, high trust creates an advantage. In fact, as evidenced by one
company, genuine trust between employer and
employee can be leveraged into long-term industry domination.

A CASE STUDY: TRUST AND
SUCCESS AT LINCOLN ELECTRIC

The Lincoln Electric Company in Cleveland
has thrived where others have failed. Situated
amidst long-abandoned factories in America's
rust belt, this manufacturer of welding equipment has sustained both tremendous profitability and its industry leadership position for several
decades.

Lincoln's product strategy has always been basic: Produce the highest quality product at the
lowest cost possible and pass the savings along to
the customer, thereby expanding demand. High
efficiency, high market share, high profit. It
sounds like the simplistic marketing plan of a
college freshman writing a paper for his first
business course. But at Lincoln, it's really that
unvarnished.

Significantly, the key that has made Lincoln's
system work since 1911 is an unswerving trust
between management and workers, a symmetric
belief that management and labor are a team
working toward a common end. Lincoln's management has built that trust, in large part, by
breaking down the barriers that so often kindle
an us-against-them mentality in workers. For
starters, at Lincoln there are no executive privi-
leges: no executive dining room, no mountain re-
treats, and no corporate jets or cars. Beyond

these symbols, and more important to workers, the compensation structure is parallel for those at the top and the bottom. Just as factory workers' pay is variable with performance, so is management's pay. When corporate performance declines, as it did in the early 1990s, executive pay goes down commensurately. All take the hit together.

All share in the gains together as well. Each year since 1934, most of Lincoln's profit has gone into a bonus pool to be divided among its approximately three thousand employees. This is not just your run-of-the-mill extra check at Christmas, though. Factory workers individually receive anywhere from a few thousand to tens of thousands of dollars from the profit-sharing plan. And workers are not only satisfied with the magnitude of the bonus, they are also satisfied that Lincoln is sharing its profits *equitably*. They believe they're receiving and will continue to receive a fair share of the company's prosperity. As such, Lincoln employees view their interests as aligned with those of management.

In addition to dismantling traditional barriers and sharing the wealth, the third ingredient in Lincoln's organizational trust formula is guaranteed lifetime employment. Anyone who has worked at Lincoln for two years or more is promised at least thirty hours of work each week. Many firms, like IBM, have made and broken such promises, but Lincoln has steadfastly honored theirs ever since 1951. Even during the drastic downturn of 1982–83 when Lincoln saw its sales volume drop 40 percent, the company was able to keep everyone employed.

Guaranteed employment is integral to the firm's success, because as management periodically updates equipment and redesigns the work system, employees do not resist. Management typically gets quick buy-in because employees fully trust that their jobs are secure.

The results of the Lincoln philosophy speak for themselves. Lincoln Electric has been the eight-hundred-pound gorilla in the industry for as long as anyone can remember. In the process, they have driven out numerous competitors, including corporate behemoth General Electric. As for Lincoln's workforce, although some employees may not love their jobs, they are committed to making the system work. This is perhaps best evidenced by their productivity levels—two to three times the national average!

The linchpin to Lincoln's extraordinary commitment and efficiency is its culture of bilateral trust, a culture that management has effected and sustained by being trustworthy.[8]

TRUST BEGETS TRUST

When it comes to building organizational trust, the principle of reaping and sowing is clearly in full operation. Trust begets trust. Distrust begets distrust.

So whether you're responsible for five people or five thousand, the move to a more trusting culture can begin entirely with you. It begins by intentionally adopting a Christlike attitude toward your subordinates and thereby permitting unconventional, trust-oriented questions to enter your decision making. Among these questions might be: "Will my decision have the effect of increasing or decreasing the trust that employees place in me?" "Will the manner in which I am reaching this decision make my employees suspicious?" And "If I were on the receiving end of this decision, would I trust that the decision-maker had my best interests in mind?"

These are powerful questions, but they are also inconvenient ones. Taking them seriously will decelerate the process and, in many cases, will entail defending your unorthodox approach to skeptical higher-ups. It's important to remember, though, that things like convenience, expediency, and political palatability tend to be the enemies of "love and faithfulness." They, in essence, represent competing paradigms for making people-management decisions.

However, in this case, these secular paradigms are competing with the Word of God, a Word that says: "Imitate Christ and build trust."

NOTES

1. This anecdote is compiled from the following sources: Bridget O'Brien, "In the Wake of Eastern Airlines' Demise, Rival Carriers Swoop in for the Pieces," *The Wall Street Journal*, 21 January 1991, B1; Bureau of National Affairs, "Machinists at Eastern Airlines Reject Settlement Package by More Than 98 Percent," *Daily Labor Reporter*, 22 September 1988, A-16; Bureau of National Affairs, "ESOP Hasn't Worked at Eastern, Executive Tells UCLA Conference," *Daily Labor Reporter*, 3 March 1988, A-2.

2. See Sandra L. Robinson and Denise M. Rousseau, "Violating the Psychological Contract: Not the Exception But the Norm," *Journal of Organizational Behavior*, 15, no. 3 (1994): 245–59. See also Alan Farnham, "The Trust Gap: Corporate America Is Split by a Gulf Between Top Management and Everybody Else—in Pay, in Perks, and in Self-Importance," *Fortune*, 4 December 1989, 56.

3. Roger C. Mayer, James H. Davis, and F. David Schoorman, "An Integrative Model of Organizational Trust," *Academy of Management Review,* 20, no. 3 (June 1995): 709–34.

4. See 2 Samuel 5–10. See also John Bright, *A History of Israel,* 3d. ed. (Philadelphia: Westminster, 1981), 195–207.

5. See Diego Gambetta, ed., *Trust* (New York: Basil Blackwell, 1988).

6. See, for example, Sandra L. Robinson, "Trust and Breach of the Psychological Contract," *Administrative Science Quarterly,* vol. 41, no. 4 (1996): 574–99.

7. Sandra L. Robinson, Matthew S. Kraatz, and Denise M. Rousseau, "Changing Obligations and the Psychological Contract: A Longitudinal Study," *Academy of Management Journal,* vol. 37, no. 1 (1994): 137–52; and Sandra L. Robinson and Elizabeth Wolfe Morrison, "Psychological Contracts and OCB: The Effects of Unfulfilled Obligations," *Journal of Organizational Behavior,* vol. 16, no. 3 (1995): 289–98.

8. This information on Lincoln Electric comes from the following sources: Randall S. Schuler, *Managing Human Resources,* 5th ed. (Minneapolis: West, 1995), 155–156, 425–438, 718–19; and "The Lincoln Electric Company," Harvard Business School case 9-376-028, (1974). The 1974 case study is available from HBS Press, Cambridge, Massachusetts, telephone: 800-545-7685.

RELIEVE EMPLOYEE STRESS

While checking on some of his bags at an airport, a traveler became very indignant with David, the curbside porter who was handling his luggage. For several minutes, he berated the young employee, criticizing everything from the pace at which he was working to the sloppiness of his uniform. He chastised David's seemingly slothful work ethic, bemoaned the dismal state of today's youth, and threatened to report David to his supervisor.

Surprisingly, throughout the tirade, the porter did not appear the least bit stressed by the abuse (an attitude that even further incensed the passenger). David simply continued his work, occasionally nodding to the repeated question: "Are you listening to me, pal?!"

After the passenger left to locate his gate, another man approached David and said: "That guy was unbelievable. How do you put up with such people?"

The porter slyly smiled, replying: "It's actually pretty easy. He's going to New York, but I'm sending his bags to Brazil!"[1]

If you don't take steps to alleviate your employees' stress, they will find a way to relieve it on their own. And seldom will their release be particularly good for business.

Before getting into the remedies, though, it is important we begin with the recognition that workplace stress is not all bad. Yes, it is true that too much stress is unhealthy for the individual and hinders the organization. It can lead to burnout, to poor customer service, to lower quality and productivity, to higher turnover, to problems off the job, and to myriad other negative outcomes. However, since it is such a powerful motivator, workplace stress in some contexts can aid an individual. It can motivate us, for example, to engage in productive behaviors that we otherwise may have neglected. To cite one of countless examples, New United Motor Manufacturing, Inc. (NUMMI), a joint venture of General Motors and Toyota, has institutionalized a team-based work process with subtle stresses that reduce employee absence. Because the system has almost no buffers in inventory or employees, "all the difficulties of one person's absence fall on those in daily contact with the absentee—the coworkers and immediate supervisor—producing an enormous peer pressure against absenteeism."[2] Employees still take days off as necessary, but illegitimate absences have gone virtually to zero.

The point is that workplace stress can work both for and against any given individual—a two-dimensional characteristic that often leads psy-

chiatrists to liken it to a rubber band. To make
the band useful, one must stretch (stress) it a bit;
however, too much stress and the band breaks.
The analogy is a perfect one, not just because it
simplifies our explanation of a complex phenom-
enon but also because it wholly comports with
Scripture's teachings on the subject. In both
Proverbs and in the Gospels, God seems to affirm
that stressors can be beneficial, while simultaneously challenging us to alleviate tensions that
have become burdensome in others' lives.

PROVERBS ON STRESS

Proverbs suggests that motivating through
stress is legitimate up to a point, but should then
be curtailed thereafter. Consider the following
two verses:

A laborer's appetite works for him;
his hunger drives him on.
(Proverbs 16:26)

A generous man will prosper;
he who refreshes others will
himself be refreshed.
(Proverbs 11:25)

Discomfort and concern about the future can
surely be stressful. Both of these verses assume
that. However, rather than condemning stress or
saying that it should be avoided, Proverbs 16:26
actually champions it. The stress of being hungry

"works for [us]," it notes. Stress is regarded as an ally because of its motivational potential: it "drives [us] on." The natural interpretation, it would seem, is that the individual who is concerned about basic needs will embrace a stronger work ethic than he would otherwise. Stated differently, stress can have a catalytic effect on our performance and on our overall contribution. However, Proverbs neither says nor implies that stress is always an attribute.

There is a bigger picture here, as one can see from juxtaposing the teaching of 16:26 with the call in 11:25 to refresh others. The Hebrew term translated as "refreshes" carries the connotation of watering, satiating, and soaking. In fact, the NRSV, the KJV, and the NASB all say that he who "waters" others will himself be "watered." Remember, water is more than just something that refreshes; it is a life-sustaining substance. It replenishes and helps living things grow. Proverbs 11:25, therefore, is not just a call to lend an occasional hand when others ask; it is a call to go above and beyond what anyone would expect. It is a call to generously water those thirsting from burdens, to satiate others' pain with encouragement, and to soak their stress in relief.

The notion that stress can "work for us" so long as it is kept in check is modeled in the very ministry of Christ. It is well-known that when Christ taught about the afterlife, He talked more about hell than He did about heaven. He conveyed in no uncertain terms that there are grave consequences to ignoring the Way (see John 14:6)—a disquieting revelation by any measure. Eternity in paradise or eternity apart from God?

What issue could generate any more trepidation than this one?

But Christ used this stress for our own good. Our consternation can motivate us to make the most important decision one can make: the decision to follow Christ. It is seemingly a divinely appointed stress designed to rescue some of us from an unspeakable future. To paraphrase Proverbs 16:26, such stress indeed "works for us."

Consistent with the proverbial instruction about stress, *after Christ beneficently used stress as a motivational tool, He took it upon Himself to keep our stress about eternity from enveloping us.* Through His sacrifice on the cross—which would guarantee salvation to all believers—He made a pathway to "refresh" us. He alleviated our stress. In terms of the earlier analogy, Jesus stretched the rubber band to make it useful, but He also reinforced it to ensure that it would not break.

STRESS: USE, BUT DO NOT ABUSE

Let's apply these two scriptural dimensions of stress to a management context. According to Proverbs, it seems that it is legitimate to use stress for the traditional function of regulating the pace, quantity, and quality of work. However, on the flip side, it is also incumbent on the Christian manager to mitigate any harmful effects of that stress. To take a practical example, institutionalizing the "stress" of negative consequences for underperformance can in many cases "work for" both employees and the organization. Better performance can operate to everyone's advantage. But in those cases where work rules and company policies unfairly burden an underperforming employee (for instance, because of inadequate training or a poor job fit), the Christian manager is to distinguish him or herself as a witness by engaging in some proactive, innovative refreshing of the employee. The manager should find a way to quash that stress while keeping organizational interests in mind.

Similarly, where an employee's stress is not work-related, the Scriptures again invite the believer to facilitate some relief. This could mean referral to counseling, development of an employee assistance program, or maybe just spending some time in conversation with the employee. Whatever the remedy, though, its effectiveness will be a function of both an attitude of concern and a willingness to get involved.

In turn, Proverbs 11:25 tells us that the manager who takes it upon him or herself to "refresh" others will also be "refreshed." Perhaps that refreshment will come in the form of more loyal employees, a more dedicated team, or lower turnover. Perhaps it will come more satisfyingly in the form of hearing God's "well done!" In either case, Proverbs teaches that alleviating employee stress is a rewarding endeavor.

STRATEGIES FOR STRESS REDUCTION

As workplace stress becomes an increasingly hot topic in the media and in the business literature, panaceas from the reasonable to the bizarre are multiplying rapidly. Companies have brought massage therapists into the workplace, permitted employees to take twenty-minute naps, paid employee sabbaticals, and even held company-sponsored water gun fights during breaks. In one particularly novel approach, Health Care and Retirement (HCR) Corporation instituted an employee "hugging policy" to drain workplace tensions and to cultivate a more family-like atmosphere on the job. If the hugger has the hugee's permission, the company advocates a warm and caring embrace.[3] "Nice job on that project, Susan. Mind if I put my arms around you?"

Like other managerial initiatives, some stress-reduction practices are effective and others are not (and still others may land a company in court for encouraging sexual harassment!). *The common thread through those that enduringly meet both employee and employer interests, though, is a manager who is genuinely sensitive to the issue and who is willing to consistently devote time and resources to stress reduction.*

When it comes to strategies for reducing stress, a compassionate, involved manager can indeed make a difference. Jim McNamara is such a manager. At age twenty-seven, McNamara purchased a small operation in southwestern Connecticut named "Redding Nursery." In the thirty-plus years since that day, Jim and his wife Sheila have built the nursery into a well-respected landscaping business that currently handles about two thousand accounts.

Notwithstanding that growth, though, the workforce is minuscule. To remain on the front lines of the operation, Jim has always limited his team to five or fewer employees. Accordingly, with all that business and so few people, these guys really *work* for a living. Despite the small workforce and an ever-expanding customer base, the nursery delivers quality service and boasts a strong balance sheet. High customer satisfaction appears in two very telling indicators: (1) Jim has rarely had to advertise, and (2) in the first three decades of owning Redding Nursery, Jim and Sheila have never had a lawyer!

Key to their success, Jim surmises, is an employee-management philosophy that follows the Golden Rule (Matthew 7:12). Jim never asks an employee to do something that he wouldn't do himself and he always tries to be sensitive to his people's concerns. Whether in setting pay, in offering health insurance, or in accommodating employee personal needs, the boss at Redding Nursery is the employees' best friend.

As a natural outgrowth of that philosophy, several years back Jim began the practice of helping employees to relax and unwind at the end of their week. Whenever Friday's work is complete, workers are invited to congregate in the boss's house for refreshments. Some weeks the Friday gatherings take place on company time, other weeks they don't. But whether they begin at 2:00 or 4:30, every Friday most of the chairs in the small circle are occupied for the voluntary meetings.

The conversation ranges from family to the upcoming weekend to Mrs. Jones's rhododendrons—from the personal to the business-related. When the conversation moves to business, Jim gladly solicits employee ideas, even to encouraging participation in decision making.

"It builds camaraderie," Jim says of the practice. "We all relax at the end of the week and they give me their input about what's going on in the field. Sometimes even former employees show up just to hang out. And at the end of every season, we take all this one step further and go to a ball-game or some other event."

It's interesting to note that it was never the intention of the Friday get-togethers to impact things like employee retention and loyalty, though the socializing has likely contributed to both of these outcomes. The meetings were simply borne of Jim's belief that each employee is to be treated respectfully, and, as such, each employee is entitled to some employer-sponsored respite from the arduous work he performs.

The family-like culture that has developed in the wake of his employee-management strategy, the owner concludes, is its own reward. "It's gratifying to create such an environment and a pleasure to manage within it." And it has driven much of Redding Nursery's growth. Indeed, Jim McNamara seems to be a living testimony to the truth of Proverbs 11:25: "A generous man will prosper; he who refreshes others will himself be refreshed."[4]

Of course, informal Friday afternoon meetings may not be transferable to every work group. Still, the managerial attitude that underlies such gatherings is. Any manager can do it. Lessening employee stress begins with one person caring enough to address the issue for his or her subordinates. Carving out some time and setting aside some petty cash to drain the pressures of work can both meaningfully affect people's lives and actively shape the culture and the commitment of a work group.

And it can have a more important effect as well. Because "refreshing others" is so uncommon and so unexpected in the contemporary workplace, it is a powerful witness to what it means to be a follower of the One who carries the burdens of every believer.

NOTES

1. Raymond McHenry, *The Best of In Other Words...* (McHenry: Houston 1996), 339.

2. M. Parker and J. Slaughter, "Management by Stress," *Technology Review,* 91, no. 1 (1988): 43. For more information on this system, see the NUMMI web site: www.mitosys.com.

3. Associated Press, "Ohio Health Care Company Embraces a Hugging Policy," *Florida Today,* 1 February 1998, E3.

4. Information on the management practices of Redding Nursery was obtained from a personal interview with Jim and Sheila McNamara on 16 July 1998.

VALUE EMPLOYEE INPUT

On an unusually cold but bright blue morning in late January, 1986, the space shuttle Challenger lifted off as scheduled. Onlookers at Cape Kennedy oohed and aahed as the earth rumbled beneath their feet and the NASA craft thundered skyward. As the vehicle cleared the tower—the point where worried engineers had feared and warned project leaders of an explosion—one whispered to another: "We've just dodged a bullet." Seventy-three seconds later, Challenger burst into flames, killing all seven astronauts onboard.

Flashback one year, to January 24, 1985. Roger Boisjoly, a senior scientist with a NASA contractor, has examined the blackened grease on a recently flown space shuttle with both perplexity and concern. As one of the nation's leading experts in O-rings and rocket seal joints, he knows that the grease on the rings, coupled with the rings' partial erosion, is, at the very least, cause for immediate testing.

Soon thereafter, Boisjoly raises the issue with both his superiors and NASA management. He suspects that the relatively cool temperature in which the shuttle had flown had the effect of hardening the rubber O-rings on the rocket booster, causing them to lose contact with their seal. (Rocket O-rings prevent leakage in much the same way as water faucet O-rings.) This, he tells management, would permit the booster's hot combustible gases to escape their chamber via the rocket joint and compromise the O-ring. The blackened grease and partial ring erosion is evidence of this chain of events, implying an unacceptable level of risk to the shuttle and its passengers.

Management asks some tough but justified questions about Boisjoly's theory, prompting him and supervisor Arnie Thompson to perform lab tests in March on the connection between low temperature and the ability of the O-rings to create a seal in the rocket booster joint. The tests confirm Boisjoly's suspicion: At a temperature of 75 degrees Fahrenheit, the primary O-rings lost contact with their seal for only 2.4 seconds, whereas at 50 degrees, they lost contact for *ten minutes*. The backup (secondary) O-ring, however, did remain sealed throughout. From this research, the two conclude that at too low a temperature, it would be possible that neither the primary nor the secondary O-ring would seal at all, thus leading to an explosion in the booster.

By midsummer, Boisjoly is all but begging both his employer and NASA for resources to further investigate the problem. He even writes to his company's vice-president of engineering to ensure that top management is aware of the problem. In this letter, he expresses the urgent concern that if the company fails to resolve the O-ring problem, "The result would be a catastrophe of the highest order—loss of human life . . ."

In late August, the vice-president of engineering responds by formally appointing a "Seal Erosion Task Team." However, of the company's 2,500 engineers, only five are allocated for the project. This is a harbinger of the level of organizational support the team, headed by Boisjoly, will receive.

For months thereafter, the intimate group of scientists do what they can to analyze the threat, but at every turn, they are frustrated by indifference. Resources are scarce, but bureaucracy abounds. Because management would not grant verbal approval for requests, the team makes glacial progress.

January 27, 1986, the day before the space shuttle Challenger's scheduled liftoff, is a bitter cold day by Florida standards. The unseasonably low temperatures—predicted to be 18 degrees near launch time—leads to several last-minute meetings to discuss the prudence of a launch. At 8:15 that evening, three teams of engineers and managers meet by teleconference to again hear from Boisjoly on his theory. Assisted by Supervisor Thompson, Boisjoly presents thirteen charts from the March experiments. Their specific recommendation is that the temperature must be at least 53 degrees for the shuttle to safely launch.

Although Boisjoly's superiors initially appeared supportive of the recommendation, a top NASA official was not, responding bluntly: "My God . . . when do you want me to launch? Next April?"

After the presentation, the four senior managers for the contractor confer. Although not a single pro-launch statement had been made by their engineers during the meeting, the group votes 4-0 to recommend launch. At 11:00, literally at the eleventh hour, the teleconference ends and the decision is telefaxed to the Kennedy Space Center. Later that evening, Boisjoly writes in his work journal: "I sincerely hope that this launch does not result in catastrophe . . . "[1]

The next day, Boisjoly witnessed in horror that very catastrophe he had predicted.

As with the assassination of President John F. Kennedy, many Americans remember precisely where they were the moment they first watched or heard about the Challenger disaster. It was a tragedy that shocked the nation, made seemingly all the more tragic by the fact that a school teacher, Christa McAuliffe, had been invited to be among the seven on the Challenger crew. We were further horrified to learn that the 1,200 students and 140 faculty from her school collectively watched the explosion on the live television broadcast. "We were rejoicing in the liftoff . . . celebrating with her," Principal Charles Foley told reporters. "Then it stopped. That's all. It just stopped."[2]

Now, with the mourning ended and many years removed from the accident, Challenger has become, among other things, a staple for business ethics courses worldwide. Indeed, many business realities contributed to management repeatedly ignoring the advice of its expert employees—most of which had to do with things like program reputation and effects on future funding if there were a delay—but notwithstanding legitimate managerial concerns, the debacle has become a classic example of ignoring the value of employee input.

This value is easy to recognize when employees are world-renowned experts in their field. However, it's also true that an employee need not be a rocket scientist to have expertise and to contribute suggestions. In fact, one could argue that those on the front lines who are in daily contact with clients, machines, the public, the technology, etc., are a constitutive resource for improving one's product, service, or work system. Moreover, some research indicates that employee participation in decision making may have effects on variables like employee morale, productivity, and turnover.[3]

Beyond human theories and arguments, though, God's Word speaks often to valuing the input of others when making decisions.

PROVERBS' ADVICE ON ADVICE

Two insightful verses on the need to receive counsel before making a decision are found in the proverbs:

*Plans fail for lack of counsel, but with
many advisers they succeed.*
(Proverbs 15:22)

*He who answers before listening—
that is his folly and his shame.*
(Proverbs 18:13)

Proverbs has a tough message for many bosses: You don't know everything. You may know your industry; you may know how the organization works or how to manage your budget. You may even have an alphabet soup of credentials following your name. But you can always learn from others.

Solicit and Welcome Advice

There are two central points about advice that the Book of Proverbs offers to us. First, Proverbs 15:22 and its close parallels (11:14; 12:15; 20:18; 24:6) encourage us to *actively solicit advice*. Seek it out, because "plans fail for lack of counsel."

Not all unilaterally designed plans will fail, of course. We know that because most executives have seen some of their lone-ranger-type projects actually come to fruition. But most of us may not have to think very hard to recall the embarrassment and frustration of plans that disintegrated because we were simply too stubborn to ask for help. Or perhaps we spurned the suggestions that were offered to us. Because we don't have all the answers, soliciting input from "many advisers," the verse tells us, leads to a greater likelihood of success.

Second, and equally important—but also equally neglected—is to *respect unsolicited advice*. In practice, when a subordinate comes to us with a suggestion, most of us will listen to it. But beneath the seemingly attentive veneer, are we really listening? Are we actually giving serious consideration to the unsolicited advice? Or are we in our minds, as Proverbs 18:13 cautions us against, answering before listening? Do we dismiss the sug-

gestion before really weighing its value? Proverbs'
instruction is to not assume that we always know
best; instead give authentic consideration to the
merits of the unsolicited advice.

Be Humble

Implicit in this advice to welcome advice is a
virtue discussed as Principle 3: be humble. Soliciting advice and respecting unsolicited advice are
acts of humility, something with which legions of
bosses struggle. Refusing counsel and answering
before listening are simply manifestations of
pride. Proverbs 13:10 makes this connection explicitly:

> *Pride only breeds quarrels,*
> *but wisdom is found in*
> *those who take advice.*
> (Proverbs 13:10)

Here, pride is set against wisdom, and wisdom
is correlated with taking advice. Although the
verse never mentions humility, the teaching is
quite patent: Have the humility to be teachable.
Set aside the prideful notion that you know it all
and seek advice. This is the godly path of the
wise.

Valuing employee advice (and all other advice,
for that matter) begins by devaluing one's complete self-sufficiency. In humility, solicit advice
from subordinates and others and respect counsel that is unsolicited. *Listen before answering.*

These are principles that could have saved seven lives in 1986.

SOLICITING IDEAS
CONFIDENTIALLY AT PILLSBURY

When it comes right down to it, respecting unsolicited advice is a personal issue entirely within one's own control. Actively soliciting employee ideas, though, is another matter.

Candor has never been the strong suit of most employees. Regardless of how many satisfaction surveys they receive and how many times they are urged to take advantage of the boss's "open door policy," it is virtually impossible to defeat the pervasive notions that (1) management will simply ignore suggestions from below, and (2) there may be some reprisal for criticisms, regardless of how constructively they are phrased.

Overcoming Employee Fears

So the practical question for the Christian manager then becomes: How does one overcome the perceived barriers to effectively implement Proverbs' advice on advice? How do you get employees to offer suggestions and to tell you what's really on their minds?

The Pillsbury Company, a Minneapolis-based food corporation, has found a way.

In 1993, Pillsbury contracted with a third party to establish a toll-free, twenty-four-hour hot line for employee comments. When an employee calls the number, he or she is first given the option to remain anonymous or to leave a name, and can then leave a comment of up to four minutes in duration. The contractor then transcribes the messages and sends them straight to the top of the organization, where every message is reviewed by the CEO, the general counsel, and the VP of human resources. The cost for the company is about three dollars per employee per year.

Once the hot line was installed, Pillsbury needed to get employees to use it. Through an aggressive wave of advertising that included the distribution of stickers and magnets, employees both became aware of the tool and gained trust in its confidentiality.

Tasting Success at Pillsbury

During its first five years of operation, employees left more than two thousand messages. Thirty-six percent concerned benefits, 18 percent were product and cost-savings ideas, 18 percent involved workplace morale issues, 7 percent dealt with the workplace environment. Another 7 percent centered on policies and procedures, and the balance were miscellaneous. What perpetuates the system and largely determines its success, though, is management follow-through. *Every question receives a response.* Answers to questions of general interest are posted on employee bulletin boards and are sometimes addressed in the *Pillsbury Today* newsletter. Individuals who leave their name get personalized feedback, typically from a local manager to whom the transcript has been forwarded. The employees are regularly reminded that the hot line is not a voting machine, but they also know that their feedback will not fall on deaf ears and will not affect their performance review.

And what of its tangible success? Pillsbury

says that the first five years of the hot line's operation generated about two hundred usable product and cost-savings ideas. Employees tend to
like the system, as does senior management since
it not only spawns worthwhile suggestions, but it
also keeps top management in touch with what
matters most to employees.[4]

Indeed, it would seem that Pillsbury has found
a recipe for valuing employee input that derives
from the scriptural cookbook: "Plans fail for lack
of counsel, but with many advisers they succeed."

BEING TEACHABLE

Scripture exhorts us to be humble enough to
be teachable, and teachable enough to learn from
those who work for us.

It is important to recognize, though, that in
implementing this teaching, no one approach is
mandated. Mechanisms for employee "input"
range from traditional suggestion boxes and
open supervisor doors to hot lines, sophisticated
surveys, and formal committees. In other words,
from the highly informal to the structured and
institutionalized.

Note that Scripture does not speak to the particulars of implementation. Rather, as is so often
the case, *God is less concerned with specific managerial processes than He is with the transformation of one's heart*. The initial attitude of many
Christian managers, unfortunately, is that virtues
can be workplace liabilities. Humility is weak-
ness, teachability is a tacit admission of inade-
quacy, and accepting input from below implies a
personal deficiency in innovation and acumen.
Both one's sinful nature and one's corporate cul-

ture perpetuate this condition, whose fruit is the destructive mind-set that one must always have the answer.

But no one does. And according to God, the supreme evaluator, that's OK. When we embrace this liberating reality—that we don't have all the answers—we have taken the first critical step in turning away from pride and corporate norms. The wise manager will complete this turnaround and genuinely value the advice of others.

NOTES

1. Russell P. Boisjoly, Ellen Foster Curtis, and Eugene Mellican, "Roger Boisjoly and the Challenger Disaster: The Ethical Dimensions," *Journal of Business Ethics*, 8, no. 4 (1989): 217–30.
2. News Services, "The Challenger Tragedy: Joy Choked Off As Christa's Pupils Watch TV," *San Diego Union and Tribune*, 29 January 1986, 1.
3. In recent decades, many researchers have tested the theory behind the contemporary employee participation movement, but their results remain inconclusive on the general question of participation's effect on performance, turnover, and satisfaction. For example, compare John L. Cotton, et al., "Employee Participation: Diverse Forms and Different Outcomes," *Academy of Management Review*, 13, no. 1 (1988): 8–22, to John A. Wagner III, "Participation's Effects on Performance and Satisfaction," *Academy of Management Review*, 19, no. 2 (1994): 312–30. Owing to this scholarly incertitude, the various findings are not presented here.
4. Gillian Flynn, "Pillsbury's Recipe is Candid Talk," *Workforce*, 77, no. 2 (February 1998): 56–59.

DEVELOP EMPLOYEE CAREERS

She knew the product, she had dealt with many of the customers, and she had a college degree. So why was she still a secretary?

That was the disconcerting question that plagued Eve Smith every day of her work life. Ms. Smith (not her real name) had aspired to work in a managerial capacity or perhaps as a sales rep for her Wichita, Kansas, employer. But the firm would not consider her for any such slot. The credentials just weren't there.

So Eve repeatedly asked to get into one of the company's training programs to fill in some gaps in her background. The infuriating response, though, had always been to hide behind company policy: Given her secretarial status, she was eligible only for training seminars that pertained to her current job. Policy dictated that she could take a word processing class, but not one on marketing.

Stuck at what she considers a dead end, Eve

has admitted to feelings of both frustration and failure. "There are some people out there who are satisfied being someone's assistant," she sighed without passing judgment. "But there are some of us who want more."[1]

Eve's experience is hardly unique. Every day, career-oriented employees complain of what appears to be managerial indifference to their desire for growth and development. And, truth be told, many of their grievances have validity. Employee career development is seldom even a blip on a manager's radar screen. There's nothing diabolical behind this; the indifference in most cases is a function of a manager's crushing workload. Confronted by daily pressures to meet deadlines, to hit production targets, and to stay on budget, who has the time to attend to such secondary concerns? Accordingly, since career development has no bearing on the crisis du jour, it gets relegated to a perpetual back-burner status, if it's on the stove at all. *Perhaps I can take care of that discussion during her next annual review,* the manager tells himself. *Or maybe,* he reasons, *the employee should deal with that issue on her own. After all, it's her career, isn't it?*

We can view it that way if we choose. But when we do, we increase the likelihood that for our own Eve Smiths, the hope for a more satisfying career will remain unfulfilled.

A PROVERB ON HOPE AND FULFILLMENT

Proverbs 13:12 acquaints us with why it's important for a manager to take some responsibility to meet the work-related aspirations of employees:

> *Hope deferred makes the heart*
> *sick, but a longing fulfilled*
> *is a tree of life.*
> (Proverbs 13:12)

The Consequences of a Sick Heart

Anyone who has ever anxiously anticipated some significant life event, only to have those hopes dashed, remembers the dreadful feeling. Ask the bride who is stood up at the altar or the mother who has just miscarried a child. Ask the student who graduates from college to the ranks of the unemployed or the young girl who does not receive the long-awaited Christmas present she secretly wished for. It can be vexing, even devastating. It is perceived as nothing short of a gross injustice, and, as such, it requires immediate answers and, better yet, a speedy remedy.

The first line of this proverb likens the feeling to a sick "heart," a word choice that was surely not cavalier. Biblical authors both in the Old and New Testament often refer to one's heart condition as an explanation for some future behavior of that individual. For example, we read in Exodus that Pharaoh's obstinate behavior toward Israel was directly attributable to God hardening his heart. Because of his calloused heart, Pharaoh refused to let the people go (4:21), refused to listen to Moses and Aaron (7:3–4), and pursued Israel into the Red Sea (14:4). In 1 Kings, immediately after Solomon received a "wise and discerning heart" (1 Kings 3:12), he made a shrewd decision (verses 16–28), and then went on to write some of Proverbs, the most considerable wisdom literature in history. And most notably, in Matthew's gospel, we see the close connection between heart and behavior in the words of Christ: "For out of the heart come evil thoughts, murder, adultery, sexual immorality, theft, false testimony, slander" (Matthew 15:19).

So when we read in Proverbs 13:12 that "hope deferred makes the heart sick," we should understand it in that context. A sick heart caused by a long-unfulfilled hope will not remain in a dormant condition; it will likely induce some action by the individual whose expectations were not met. The feeling will do more than just fester internally, the proverb says. *Deferred hopes will ultimately manifest themselves as external, observable behaviors.*

The Joy of a Longing Fulfilled

In examining the flip side of this teaching, the second phrase of Proverbs 13:12 paints a sharp contrast to the first. A fulfilled longing is called "tree of life," a term that traces its roots to the Garden of Eden: "In the middle of the garden were the tree of life and the tree of the knowledge of good and evil" (Genesis 2:9). Significantly, an earlier proverb terms wisdom a "tree of life" (Proverbs 3:18), and the term also appears in the last book of the Bible, with Christ Himself promising the faithful "the right to eat from the tree of life, which is in the paradise of God" (Revelation 2:7). In Scripture, the "tree of life" is a metaphor for eternal life.

The latter message of the proverb, then, is *that a "longing fulfilled" can seem like heaven to those who experience it.* Contrasting this with the first line of the verse, we are presented with the choice of extremes (a literary device that makes a proverb's wisdom quite memorable). As usual, we are challenged to see two paths before us. Defer one's hope and you will provoke some negative behavior; fulfill it, and that person will be overjoyed.

THE CONNECTION TO CAREER DEVELOPMENT

What are the practical implications of this instruction for managers? The teaching implies much more than a reminder to identify and meet employees' needs. Such issues as fair pay, job security, health benefits, a safe work environment, and adequate time off are essential to employees, but they are merely basic needs. Proverbs 13:12 is a specific call to attend to work-related "longings" of our subordinates—higher-order needs and desires.

For many workers, foremost among those things that qualify as longings is an aspiration for personal and career development. Many, like Eve Smith, view work as more than just a means to a financial end; rather, work and career provide avenues for people to exercise and develop their God-given talents, to reach that elusive top rung of "self-actualization" and fulfillment, described by noted psychologist Abraham Maslow as the highest need in his hierarchy of needs model, and to lead more purposeful lives. Eve Smith's job did none of those things and, accordingly, this "hope deferred"—this unfulfilled longing—took its toll on her commitment and on her feelings of self-worth.

Eve's experience offers anecdotal evidence for the truth of Proverbs 13:12, but empirical evidence affirms it. In particular, researchers have investigated the connection between an individual's career goals and an organization's needs. Their conclusion: When an organization satisfies employee goals—when it attends to career development and creates pathways for internal mobility—the employee responds very positively, often by investing time in the training necessary to take on more responsibilities.[2] The employee is willing to meet organizational needs (e.g., higher productivity and quality, more flexibility) in return for a fulfilled longing.

However, what the proverb calls "hope deferred" has been empirically linked to negative outcomes. Conflict between the employee career goals and the organization's willingness or ability to satisfy those goals culminates in lower job satisfaction and poorer performance.[3] It creates a sick heart that, in turn, influences the employee's contribution and can also lead to turnover. Having recognized these consequences, organizations of all sizes have made employee career development a priority.

WHAT IF UPWARD
MOBILITY IS NOT POSSIBLE?

But we also must recognize that upward mobility is not possible in some situations. Developing an internal career path for all employees remains difficult due to the elimination of many middle-management positions and the trend toward less hierarchy in flattening organizations. Moreover, in smaller organizations there is often nowhere for one to be promoted, except to the executive level. There are also scenarios where, even though promotion is possible, an employee has simply plateaued and does not have the aptitude for higher level work. Do these realities render the proverbial wisdom inoperable?

Developing New Skills

They don't. In each of these situations, employees still have longings for meaningful work and for intrinsically rewarding careers. And they usually have untapped potential as well. Accordingly, in cases where upward movement is precluded, a manager might consider the concept of "career enrichment," a paradigm that focuses not on promotability, but rather on encouraging employees to "grow in place."

Chevron Corporation has developed such a system. When economic pressures forced the petroleum exploration and refining company to lay off approximately eight thousand employees in the late 1980s and early 1990s, its career development system was effectively torpedoed. Chevron could no longer credibly promise "career development" because that implied upward growth. They therefore changed their emphasis to career enrichment, a system by which employees are encouraged to develop new skills and to make lateral moves that can enhance both job satisfaction and employee effectiveness.

Training and transfers are voluntary, and no salary increases or promotions are guaranteed, but the recently implemented system does permit Chevron workers to pursue intrinsically rewarding activities.[4] Career enrichment is no doubt a compromise solution, but it appears to be optimal given Chevron's competitive constraints.

Using a Job Rotation Program

This same principle of simultaneously addressing employee longings and organizational needs is the basis of formal "job rotation" programs, a system where workers periodically rotate from one job to another at the same level. Long championed as a way to lessen boredom and increase motivation, job rotation may also meet some employee needs for career satisfaction. A recent study of the rotation program at Eli Lilly and Company found just that; the employees' voluntary job rotation at Lilly enhanced and broadened the skills of the workforce, while improving the career satisfaction of those employees who chose to participate in the program.[5] Indeed, some costs arise in such a system, including employee time to learn, training costs, and errors from those undertaking new jobs, and work flow is typically disrupted. But these are really investments. The payout accrues to both the organization, primarily in the form of a more highly skilled workforce, and to the employee, who experiences job and career satisfaction.

Job rotation and the broader concept of growing in place are not necessarily a panacea in employee development. But where promotability is limited, such approaches do afford employees some control over the extent to which their career longings might be fulfilled.

KNOW AND RESPOND TO EMPLOYEE ASPIRATIONS

To cultivate a culture of employee commitment, managers should show employees that the organization is committed to them. One way to do this is by investing some time asking subordinates about their career aspirations. A more powerful way is to actually design customized programs for employees and to assist them with the implementation. In doing so, this communicates to employees that they are long-term players. It can give them a sense of belonging. And it can restore meaningfulness to one's work, an outcome that benefits productivity in ways that compensation simply cannot.

There is genuine value in being sensitive to the career aspirations of employees at all levels—value for both the employee and the organization. Conversely, insensitivity and indifference generate detrimental results of their own. Proverbs teaches that a manager is well-served by remembering that hope deferred and longings fulfilled have significantly different aftereffects. By satisfying the longings, the manager gives the employee greater hope, and the company reaps a more committed, more contented worker.

NOTES

1. Guy Boulton, "Secretaries Aspiring to Move Up Often Go Nowhere," *Houston Chronicle*, 5 July 1991, 3.
2. See, for example, Marilyn K. Quaintance, "Internal Placement and Career Management" in Wayne F. Cascio, ed., *Human Resource Planning, Employment and Placement* (Washington, D. C.: Bureau of National Affairs, 1989), 2-200 to 2-235.
3. Jeanne M. Brett and Anne H. Reilley, "On the Road Again: Predicting the Job Transfer Decision," *Journal of Applied Psychology*, 73, no. 4 (1988): 614–20; Stanley B.

Malos and Michael A. Campion, "An Options-Based Model of Career Mobility in Professional Service Firms," *Academy of Management Review*, 20, no. 3 (1995): 611–44.

4. Shari Caudron, "HR Revamps Career Itineraries," *Personnel Journal*, 43, no. 4 (April 1994): 64.

5. Michael A. Campion, Lisa Cheraskin, and Michael J. Stevens, "Career-Related Antecedents and Outcomes of Job Rotation," *Academy of Management Journal*, 37, no. 6 (1994): 1518–42.

PART FOUR

EVALUATING
AND
REWARDING
PERFORMANCE

MEASURE PERFORMANCE VALIDLY

One by one, agents of the Internal Revenue Service took a seat behind a partition that screened them from public view, each testifying to more grievous practices than the one before. One by one, in voices that were electronically altered to further hide their identity, they told the U. S. Senate Finance Committee horror stories of being pressured by superiors to overzealously enforce the law and to deprive taxpayers of their rights. When it was over, six witnesses had told corroborating tales of a federal agency out of control.

Then it came time for the IRS commissioner to respond. Rather than dispute the allegations, though, Commissioner Michael P. Dolan contritely testified: "I don't come here in denial. It distresses me greatly to see the mistakes we have made."

The extent of those "mistakes" was officially released a few months later by the newly installed commissioner, Charles Rossotti. Rossotti's internal report indicated that a primary culprit in the agency's missteps was its performance measurement system. The agency, Rossotti said, had rated its employees on their aggressiveness in collecting delinquent taxes and in seizing property. Moreover, it ranked its thirty-three district offices based on the amount of money each brought in. Agents received incentives to both inflate their personal performance rating and the national ranking of their district office, leading to browbeating and abuse of citizens who were delinquent in paying federal income taxes. However, the internal agency report noted, the performance evaluation system did not measure the level or quality of service provided to taxpayers.[1]

This 1997 audit of the auditors culminated in the very public humiliation of the Internal Revenue Service and its top management. Admittedly, their goal may have been laudable—collecting taxes that were due—but the mechanism by which they pursued that goal was fatally flawed.

It is difficult to overstate the power of an organization's performance measurement system. As the IRS experience makes clear, the manner in which management measures performance directly impacts employee behavior. It can establish their priorities, determine their motivation, regulate the quality and speed of their work, and influence whether they remain in the organization.

In fact, this system is so pivotal that when it fails, many other employee management systems fail in its wake. For instance, how does the company pay for performance if it does not properly measure performance? Moreover, without properly measuring performance, on what basis does a manager promote or lay off? How does a manager defend performance-related discipline? And how can a manager offer constructive feedback on performance and make appropriate training and development decisions?

The answer: blindly. Yet, although performance measurement is an essential tool to implement many business objectives (like collecting back taxes),[2] the time and expense required to measure performance accurately often preclude an effective system design. Accordingly, the employee evaluation process has been duly criticized; it remains fodder for comic strips and, now, congressional hearings.

"Valid" is the contemporary term for saying that a system measures what it's supposed to measure. And valid measurement is a concept that God thought important enough to address in His Word.

PROVERBS ON VALID MEASUREMENT

In a proverb containing a strong image and an even stronger verb, we learn a key principle about accurate measurement:

The Lord abhors dishonest scales,
but accurate weights are his delight.
(Proverbs 11:1)

A Form of Deception and Theft

The mentioning of "dishonest scales" is practical, not fanciful, for in King Solomon's day the trade system relied on precious metals such as gold, silver, and copper as mediums of exchange.

Transactions required that a merchant weigh a customer's metals on a scale consisting of two pans that were suspended by cords from the ends of a horizontal beam. The merchant would place a known quantity of weight on one pan and the metals on the other until the scale balanced.

This approach to commerce, of course, afforded merchants ample opportunity to bilk their customers. Although most weights bore a visible inscription indicating their magnitude, the customer had no guarantee that the merchant's inscription was accurate. Traveling tradesmen, therefore, made a practice of carrying their own weights with them on business. Others, though, could easily be duped by unscrupulous merchants employing "dishonest scales."

Through their experiences (or those of their friends), the original audience knew exactly what the proverb meant when alluding to "dishonest scales." This was intentional mismeasurement and therefore a form of deception and theft. It cheated a person out of his or her money. For this reason, Proverbs 11:1 tells us, it is a practice that the Lord "abhors."

Consequences of Underrating—and Overrating—Employees

In the same way, when a manager mismeasures human performance, whether intentionally or not, he is in essence using a dishonest scale. Sometimes he will *underevaluate* an individual's work performance, therefore devaluing one's contribution. The results of underevaluation usually are reducing one's raise and limiting advancement opportunities. Underevaluation can

even, in extreme cases, lead to termination. It is
no stretch to say, then, that when a manager un-
derrates an employee's performance, that manager's "scale" cheats the employee out of the most
valuable job outcomes.

Proverbs 3:27 supplements this point. It says:

Do not withhold good from those
who deserve it, when it is
in your power to act.
(Proverbs 3:27)

The verse speaks plainly to the manager who
negligently or otherwise "lowballs" a subordinate's productivity. The manager who underval-
ues an employee's work is withholding something
"good"—a better appraisal (and its accompany-
ing outcomes)—from one who deserves it. It follows that the Christian manager, when he or she
has the "power to act" in rating subordinates, is
instructed to vigilantly avoid underevaluation.

However, *overevaluating* employee performance is no better, as this can in effect cheat one's
organization. As noted earlier, the performance
evaluation system feeds all other employee management functions. Thus, systematically overevaluating people can unduly increase compensation
costs, hamstring the identification of the best and
brightest for promotion, undermine training and
development initiatives, encourage employees to
continue making the same mistakes, and create
severe managerial and legal difficulties in termi-

nations or reductions in force.

In current jargon, such overevaluation is termed "leniency bias," a prejudice toward being too easy during a performance review. Three thousand years ago, Proverbs' term was "pampering."

---

*If a man pampers his servant
from youth, he will bring
grief in the end.*
(Proverbs 29:21)

Whether called *pampering* or *leniency bias,* the consequences remain negative. Yet in spite of the potential "grief" to the organization precipitated by such leniency, it continues to be among the chief enemies of measuring performance validly.

The practice is, however, somewhat understandable. Managers typically view performance evaluation as a mundane, administrative task that is at best a time drain and more likely a burden. Not only does it involve the twin evils of forms and meetings, but employees can get pretty touchy about negative feedback (especially if one's pay raise, promotion, or livelihood is on the line). Additionally, in many scenarios objective measures of individual performance are simply unavailable for assessment. So managers often anticipate the evaluation process with dread, an attitude that is captured trenchantly by the title of a 1996 front page article in *The Wall Street Journal*: "Annual Agony: It's Time to Evaluate Your Work, and All Involved Are Groaning."[3]

It is no wonder, then, that so many managers opt for leniency bias and give almost everyone high performance marks. It's expedient, it preserves relationships, and it requires no defense. Everybody's doing a great job. Now let's get on to more important things.

The Christian manager should recognize that this is not necessarily how God sees the evaluation process. As Proverbs 11:1 reminds us, God takes "delight" when we, in His name, use "accurate weights" in measuring things that are important to others—things like individual performance on the job. Accordingly, it is to the implementation of this teaching that we now briefly turn.

MEASURING PERFORMANCE MORE VALIDLY

It's easy to get lost in all the approaches to measuring and managing performance that have come down the pike in recent years. In both academic and popular books you can read about such systems as "360 reviews," "forced distributions," "management by objectives," and "behaviorally anchored ratings." Moreover, many of the largest corporations in the world use such approaches for evaluation. However, the relative speed at which new performance measurement ideas turn over makes managers justifiably suspicious about the long-term utility of whatever is currently in vogue.

For this reason, rather than elevate any one approach as a model, presented below are some enduring guidelines that any manager can use to measure performance more validly.[4]

Identify the Target

In 1933, a bowler named Bill Knox requested that a screen be placed across a bowling lane to obscure his view of the pins. Then Bill bowled ten frames as the curious public and reporters looked on. From an angle, they saw all the action; the bowler could only hear the pins fall.

Evaluating performance without seeing the target is a little like sitting behind Bill at the scorer's table and trying to guess how many pins Bill knocked down on each successive throw. Unable to see the pins, the scorer is bound to make mistakes. In the same way, a manager cannot reliably determine whether a subordinate is hitting a certain target until the manager has an unobscured view of that target. The implication is that the (1) tasks, (2) behaviors, and (3) expected results associated with each job should be enumerated for the one doing the rating. The collection of this information, typically called "job analysis," is usually the duty of the human resource department (HR). However, it is one of those functions that HR knows should be done but, because of budget and staffing constraints, seldom gets around to doing.[5]

This neglect, of course, does not eliminate the need to evaluate. Managers still must identify the target performance before drawing conclusions about the extent to which the target has been hit. In many organizations, then, to measure performance more validly may require that the rating manager assume the responsibility of conducting the job analysis for each job for which he or she has supervisory authority.

There is no one best way to do this, but clearly

the more formal, more thorough analyses of jobs generate more accurate data and clearer performance targets than do "armchair" methods. Thus, developing and using employee questionnaires and group interviews tend to be superior to a manager's casual recollection of major job tasks and duties. Moreover, the job analysis should be updated as new business strategies warrant that jobs evolve, merge, or otherwise change.

Disregard this first step toward validly measuring performance, and you are scoring in the dark. How many pins did Bill Knox hit on that day in 1933? Few visually impaired scorers would have ever guessed that he bowled a perfect game![6]

Keep a Record for Each Subordinate

Who hasn't walked out of a performance review meeting thinking that the boss has a selective memory? Or perhaps no memory that predates that particular month?

In most organizations, employee performance is measured annually or semiannually. A lot can happen in that time, but no one who is charged with recalling information for every subordinate can dependably do so without having kept records of their performance. Without documentation, attempting to periodically measure the performance of one employee is like taking a test in school after a full semester of taking no notes. It's like trying to explain the minister's sermon points for the past few months without ever having written a word about them. Now multiply that by several tests or several ministers and we get a sense of the folly of evaluating subordinates' performances without having kept any records. At some point, it becomes more conjecture than history.

For decades, the research has concluded that acquiring and storing information about employees improves the validity of the performance measurement process.[7] One practical recommendation from this growing body of research is that managers keep a diary or journal of subordinate performance. Both lab and field experiments have demonstrated that performance diaries not only increase both recall and rating accuracy, but they also temper leniency bias and other biases that are discussed below.[8] Furthermore, the studies say, diaries organized by employee (that is, one section for each subordinate) are superior to those organized by task or those that are unorganized.

The commonsense conclusion is that to assist your recall about employees and to maximize validity, consider adopting the habit of keeping close records of subordinate performance.

Beware of Bias

Even where a manager clearly identifies the performance targets and diligently chronicles employee progress toward those targets, a valid measurement is still threatened by the many "biases" that are endemic to the human condition. Much empirical work exists, yet the central conclusions generally reduce to something we all know intuitively: Intentional and unintentional errors by the rater often encroach on the accuracy of performance evaluation.

We have already discussed "leniency bias" as it relates to validity, but beyond this exists a host of other biases that jeopardize valid measurement. Table 4 presents a synopsis of the most common

Table 4

COMMON BIASES IN PERFORMANCE APPRAISAL

Type of Bias	Definition
Double Standard	A commonly known problem whereby a manager uses different criteria to rate similarly situated subordinates
Recency Bias	The error of according more weight to recent performance and paying little attention to the balance of the employee's record
Primacy Bias	Similar to recency bias, this is the error of according more weight to the first information one has about an employee than to other information. In this case, a manager makes an initial judgment about the employee after the first impression, and from there on, rather than objectively gathering performance information, the manager tends to store only information that supports the initial judgment.
Leniency Bias	An often-intentional error whereby all subordinates are rated too leniently
Sequencing or Contrast Effects	This occurs when the manager's rating of an employee is influenced by the quality of the previously rated employee. An average performer compared to a weak performer will appear to be outstanding, but when sequenced behind a strong performer, the average employee will be perceived as poor.
Halo Error	This happens when an employee is so outstanding in one respect that a manager rates his or her performance as high on all dimensions. The employee essentially has a "halo" and, in the eyes of the rating manager, the employee can do no wrong.

Type of Bias	Definition
Horn Error	As the name implies, this is the flip side of halo error. The employee's negative performance in one area unjustly influences his or her rating in all other performance areas.
Central Tendency Bias	The inclination on the part of some managers to rate all subordinates as average, when in reality, their performance varies
Rater Prejudice	This occurs when performance ratings are influenced by criteria like race, gender, age, religion, ethnicity, seniority, and other arbitrary classifications.

biases.

Whenever human beings are evaluating human beings, there is a vast potential for bias. This can be an especially damaging and expensive problem because, no matter how sophisticated the rest of one's performance measurement system, if it is not used properly at the moment of decision, the entire system fails.[9] Moreover, since most of these rater errors are committed unconsciously, they are unlikely to be corrected without a deliberate attempt to do so. Accordingly, to improve the validity of any performance measurement, *one should not only be aware of the potential for bias, but actively guard against it when rating subordinates*.

THE ROLE AND EFFORT
OF THE INDIVIDUAL MANAGER

Regardless of how the evaluation system formally operates in one's organization, valid measurement of subordinates' performances is an issue that depends largely on each individual manager. That's good news for the Christian who sees it as God's will that people be rated fairly and accurately.

However, this involves a significant time investment. It takes time to analyze jobs, to keep this information current, to keep records on employee performance, and to consciously reject the potential biases. But this is the nature of being a witness in the workplace. Investing an above-average amount of time in one's people is part of the Christian difference, part of the sacrifice inherent in the faith.

It is therefore to His glory that we regularly calibrate our instruments and scrutinize our measurement criteria—our "weights" in the ancient vernacular. Christian scales are honest and valid scales.

NOTES

1. This anecdote compiled from the following sources: Rob Wells, "Concealed Agents Tell of IRS Abuses," *Houston Chronicle*, 26 September 1997, 1; Ralph Vartabedian, "IRS Admits It Ranked Staff Members by Aggressiveness," *Los Angeles Times*, 14 January 1998, D1; David E. Rosenbaum, "Internal Audit Confirms Abusive IRS Practices," *The New York Times*, 14 January 1998, A14.
2. For more information on the relationship between performance measurement and strategy, see Richard W. Beatty, "Competitive Human Resource Advantage Through the Strategic Management of Performance," *Human Resource Planning*, 12, no. 3 (Summer 1989): 179–94.
3. Timothy D. Schellhardt, "Annual Agony: It's Time to Evaluate Your Work, and All Involved Are Groaning,"

The Wall Street Journal, 11 November 1996, A1.

4. Some of the better works in the area of performance measurement and management include H. John Bernardin and Jeffrey S. Kane, *Performance Appraisal: A Contingency Approach to System Development and Evaluation,* 2nd ed. (Boston: PWS Kent, 1993); Frank J. Landy and James L. Farr, *The Measurement of Work Performance: Methods, Theory and Applications* (New York: Academic Press, 1983); and H. John Bernardin and Richard W. Beatty, *Performance Appraisal: Assessing Human Behavior at Work* (Boston: Kent, 1984).

5. Job analysis is typically considered the cornerstone of a well-designed employee-management system. It not only identifies the criteria for evaluating performance, but it also supports legitimate recruitment standards, valid hiring criteria, valid training and development targets, internally equitable wage rates, and defensible rationales for promotion, discipline, and discharge.

6. Recounted in M.R. DeHaan II, *Our Daily Bread,* a monthly devotional published by RBC Ministries (Grand Rapids), 4 August 1992.

7. Among the earliest work in this area are Robert M. Guion, *Personnel Testing* (New York: McGraw-Hill, 1965) and H. John Bernardin and C. S. Walter, "Effects of Rater Training and Diary Keeping on Psychometric Error in Ratings," *Journal of Applied Psychology,* 62, no. 1 (1977): 64–69.

8. Angelo S. DeNisi, Tina L. Robbins, and Thomas P. Cafferty, "Organization of Information Used for Performance Appraisals: Role of Diary-Keeping," *Journal of Applied Psychology,* 74 , no. 1 (1989): 124–29; Angelo S. DeNisi and Lawrence H. Peters, "Organization Of Information in Memory and the Performance Appraisal Process: Evidence from the Field," *Journal of Applied Psychology,* 81, no. 6 (1996): 717–38.

9. For the classic articulation of this problem, see Frank J. Landy and James L. Farr, "Performance Rating," *Psychological Bulletin,* 87, no. 1 (1980): 72–97.

DELIVER CRITICISM WITH CARE

Willie Woods, an electrician and radio repairman for the city of Los Angeles, was not happy with the letter he had just received from his boss. The notice read that he was to appear at an internal hearing to formally respond to questions about the quality of his work.

Six months earlier at his annual review, Woods's supervisors had raised similar questions, and several times since then Woods had been warned about his performance. Apparently Woods became irate at a few of those discussions. One ended with Woods throwing a chair across the room; during another one, he openly tore up the evaluation sheet. A third time he sat sullen and silent as his supervisors urged him to shape up.

Now, facing a hearing that could result in termination, Woods sought recourse in the most ruthless manner possible. At 10 A.M. on July 19, 1995, Woods walked into the Erwin Piper Techni-

cal Center, his place of employment, to confront
management about what his union rep described
as a feeling of "being picked on and singled out."
After an initial exchange of angry words, Woods
went to his locker and returned moments later
with a Glock 9 mm semiautomatic pistol. He lo-
cated office supervisor Anthony Gain, the city's
most veteran employee with fifty-three years of
service, pointed the gun at him and fired. Woods
then turned, spied supervisor Marty Wakefield,
and fired again.

Descending one flight of stairs, he next sought
out his immediate supervisors, James Walton
and Neil Carpenter. Both were in the office that
day. Both were mercilessly gunned down, one in
an office, one in a hallway.

Two police officers from the Los Angeles Police
Department's gang unit, who were in the building
on other business, followed the sounds of gun-
fire, tracking Woods to an open area in the back
of the building. Woods surrendered to them without incident and was later sentenced to life in
prison. None of the four victims made it to the
hospital alive.[1]

The carnage in a Los Angeles office building
graphically illustrates a basic reality in managing
employee performance: Delivering negative feedback is always a precarious endeavor. Although
relatively few employees ever go this ballistic,
most do experience anxiety and anger in criticism's wake. The rebuke goes to the heart of their
egos. Many employees feel a negative evaluation
embarrasses them; they often perceive it as unfair or inconsiderate, and, as discussed in Principle 13, it can cost them both valuable rewards

and job security. And so, sometimes constructively, but often destructively, they respond.

A recent Temple University study confirmed the pervasiveness of the problem. In a survey of 151 Philadelphia-area managers, 98 percent reported some type of aggression in response to negative feedback they had delivered. The behaviors ranged from the silent treatment to stalking, with two-thirds of the worker reactions being primarily verbal in nature.[2]

But even though addressing underachieving employees is uncomfortable for both manager and employees, from a performance perspective it must be done. Additionally, from a safety perspective, it must be done diplomatically. In the 1990s the media reported more than two dozen high-profile workplace killings.[3]

Thus employers are increasingly inviting consultants into the workplace to help managers deliver negative feedback more effectively and carefully. For those who prefer the most transcendent brand of advice, though, there is an abundance available and free of charge from the Divine Consultant.

PROVERBS ON IMPARTING
NEGATIVE FEEDBACK

Proverbs offers us three connected teachings on imparting criticism in the workplace. For those who must put it into practice, it guides us in what to do before, during, and after communicating the problem to a subordinate.

Before Communicating the Problem

Prior to ever speaking a word of criticism,

Proverbs 20:5 reminds us about the attitude of humility and patience that we should bring to the table:

The purposes of a man's heart
are deep waters, but a man
of understanding draws them out.
(Proverbs 20:5)

Why has someone underperformed? Why has he been absent too often? What is the reason for her insubordination? Managers continually assume they have the answers to these questions and then unilaterally act upon those assumptions. But this approach may be impetuous, the Scriptures suggest. As managers, we do not always have the answers.

"The purposes of a man's heart"—his plans, his rationales, and his motives in the original language—"are deep waters." The latter term appears often in the Old Testament to connote mystery and unfathomability. Something resting in deep water is hidden and hard to discover. Solomon used this metaphor to indicate that the true rationale for someone's behavior may not be easy to discern. In the New Testament, the apostle Paul added a similar caution: "For who among men knows the thoughts of a man except the man's spirit within him?" (1 Corinthians 2:11).

Certainly in a work setting, a manager has limits. A boss's limited exposure to this individual may prevent him or her from observing mitigating factors. Therefore, the prudent manager avoids hasty conclusions. He chooses instead to *humbly assume that there may exist a reason for the subordinate's action that he has not considered*. It is on this assumption that one should commence discussions with problem employees.

As managers and as Christians, our next step, the verse says, is to patiently explore those murky waters. Although this is a complex task, one indeed has a responsibility to identify the root causes and motivations. According to the proverb, "a man of understanding draws them out."

Throughout Proverbs, the "man of understanding" or "of knowledge" is one who respects and reveres God and seeks to follow His path. (For example, see 15:21, 32.) Verse 20:5b reveals to us, then, that an individual with such attributes can, in fact, persevere to draw out those purposes—to bring hidden motives to the surface—as one might draw water from a deep well. It is possible. But, recalling the truth of the first half of the proverb, *such a task first requires we draw out the waters with both the humility and patience to listen and to care*. The manager should approach any rebuke of a subordinate with the mind-set that this will be a conversation rather than a lecture. The objective is to have a forbearing inquiry instead of an immediate reprimand.

So the thrust of the verse is this: Before the believer ever delivers a word of criticism, he or she lays a constructive foundation by adopting the proper attitude.

While Communicating the Problem

If one does adopt that attitude, implementing the next teaching is quite natural. Proverbs advises us to remember that when it comes time to speak with the subordinate, there is power in the words we use:

---

*Reckless words pierce like a
sword, but the tongue
of the wise brings healing.*
(Proverbs 12:18)

One's choice of words has the power to either escalate or to ameliorate. That is, how we communicate our concern and dissatisfaction can largely determine the trajectory of the conversation: more intense or more cordial. If at any point one recklessly abandons a Christlike attitude, allowing one's attitudes or emotions—perhaps frustration, aggressiveness, or revenge—free reign to "pierce like a sword," the discussion can quickly degenerate into something counterproductive. The subordinate usually strikes back, often later and covertly, with his or her own dagger. Workers' tactics can range from reducing their efforts and poisoning the culture with complaints and gossip, to pilfering from the organization or engaging in any number of other undesirable activities. Whatever their tactics, people find ways to "even the score" with their bosses, thereby escalating the conflict.

If, on the other hand, one is more careful in

word choice and in tone—a disposition that flows
from the attitude discussed above—one unleashes
the power to ameliorate, even to "bring healing."
This is wisdom's path, the path of diplomacy. In
similar proverbs, it is the path of even-tempered-
ness (e.g., Proverbs 17:27) and gentleness (e.g.,
Proverbs 15:1). And this is the path that James, in
his typical no-nonsense fashion, pointed us toward when he warned: "If anyone considers himself religious and yet does not keep a tight reign on
his tongue, he deceives himself and his religion is
worthless" (James 1:26).

In the act of delivering negative feedback,
then, reject the recklessness that may be innate
and instead speak with what the proverb calls
"the tongue of the wise."

After Communicating the Problem

Once the boss has determined a problem exists
and has sought its root cause, what follows is the
question of remedy. Ordinarily, a boss will tell the
subordinate what he or she expects in the future
and perhaps relate some consequences of non-
compliance, but Proverbs 29:19 says that this
may not always be sufficient:

---

*A servant cannot be corrected
by mere words; though he
understands, he will not respond.*

Many know the truth of this verse from frustrating experience with repeat offenders. The ex-

pectations set in November's appraisal interview may seem a distant memory by New Year's. The better approach, the verse implies, is to follow up with something beyond "mere words."

Depending on the situation, this could involve almost anything from the more heavy-handed (e.g., demotions, closer supervision, last-chance write-ups) to the more developmental (such as retraining, rehabilitation, mentoring). As noted in Principles 8 and 12, a strong case can be made for the second approach, but as Principle 19 will detail, Scripture does not mandate that employees be retained indefinitely. Accordingly, there's no mathematical formula here for remediation; rather, one should craft a remedy in the intersection of both organizational and employee needs. Importantly, though, it is wise to use something more than "mere words" to effect that remedy.

SOME TIPS FROM
RESEARCH AND PRACTICE

A Consensus Among Textbooks, Journals, and Magazines

In broad strokes, Scripture offers counsel on delivering negative feedback. As we've seen, it furnishes general principles on attitude, diplomacy, and remedial action which imply, but do not elaborate upon, the particulars of their day-to-day implementation.

By contrast, the secular literature in this area does just the opposite, tending to focus more on daily practice than on principles. And for a refreshing change, the textbooks, scholarly journals, and practitioner magazines all seem to advance similar advice on the how-to's of delivering negative feedback.[4] What's even more refreshing is that these practical conclusions appear to be wholly consistent with the proverbial paradigm, making them especially noteworthy for the Christian manager.

Ten Tips for Delivering Negative Feedback

The ten elements for delivering negative feedback that are most commonly cited in this literature are as follows:

1. *Do it privately.* To publicly criticize an employee's work or behavior is to humiliate the employee. Moreover, in our litigious society, it can even lead to defamation suits. Contrary to the practice of offering praise, which should be done publicly whenever possible (Principle 15), discussions about one's deficiencies should remain private.

2. *Do it personally.* It is usually a mistake to deliver criticisms by phone, E-mail, or some other impersonal vehicle. Although these are tempting options given the uncomfortable nature of the discussion, face-to-face conversations allow the manager to observe the employee's body language (which is often far more telling than what one verbalizes). This may assist the manager in the sometimes arduous task of identifying root problems. Similarly, personal discussion permits the employee to more clearly observe the manager's concern for both the organization and the employee.

3. *Get right to the point.* Most employees can

sense when their boss has a problem with them. Therefore, when the boss calls in an employee, but then tiptoes around what's really on his or her mind, it is both transparent and frustrating for the employee.

4. *Present the negative feedback in the context of positive performance.* Especially in annual performance review meetings, it is essential that the employee understand that his or her manager sees not just the deficiencies, but also the employee's contribution to the organization. To communicate this, a standard managerial line might be: "I think that you're doing great with 88 percent of the work I've assigned you. What we're going to talk about in the next few minutes, though, is the other 12 percent." Outside of formal meetings, the same principle applies. When disciplining or correcting a subordinate, look for ways to contrast the negative behavior with something positive in the employee.

5. *Speak in terms of "I," not "you."* Speaking in the first person is an invaluable tool for minimizing employee defensiveness. Structure your criticisms in terms of how you, the manager, feel, rather than what the subordinate has done. A statement like "I have some concerns about your sales numbers" tends to be less offensive to the receiving ears than "You are not making the sales numbers we need." Similarly, "I'm not understanding this section of your report" is more palatable than "You're not making sense in this section of your report." The first approach communicates essentially the same infor-

mation, but it puts some onus on the critiquing manager, rather than heaping it all on the subordinate.[5]

6. *Be specific.* Abstract criticisms (e.g., "You're performing well below average") do not serve a manager's ends nearly as well as more specific feedback. Rather than categorizing the performance ("well below average"), be specific about what is expected and contrast this with objective facts about what the employee has or has not accomplished. Identifying for the employee this gap between management's expectations and current performance brings into sharper focus the problem that must be addressed. Moreover, it becomes the basis for a more constructive discussion of how to bridge that gap.

7. *Stick to the facts.* Sticking to the facts is to be objective and avoid speculative judgments about the causes of misbehavior or underperformance. Instead, ask the employee about the reasons for the behavior/performance and then actively listen to the response.

8. *Don't twist the knife.* In any one discussion, there is no need to repeat criticisms. The employee gets the idea. Furthermore, if possible, stick to one problem per conversation and avoid resurrecting old problems previously resolved. Employees often perceive such piling on as unnecessary and unfair.

9. *Jointly craft a solution.* After presenting the negative feedback, involve the employee in solving the problem. An employee who has helped craft a solution may be more com-

mitted to effecting it than one who has a solution thrust upon him or her. Pinpoint the problem and set up some mutually agreeable goals as a baseline against which to evaluate future performance. Also, if appropriate, jointly design a development plan to shape the employee in the proper direction.

10. *Offer feedback continuously*. Feedback is a tool that should be used more than once or twice a year. In fact, it should ideally be a seamless function. Accordingly, when one sees a subordinate doing something wrong (or right), one should let him or her know about it immediately to correct (or reinforce) the behavior.

A FIRST STEP: THE PROPER ATTITUDE

Negative feedback is elemental to enhancing employee performance. If one does not identify and discuss the areas that require improvement, how can a manager really expect employees to improve?

We have presented ten tips based on findings of various studies. But no matter how much exposure a manager has to this secular wisdom, one is always in jeopardy of ignoring or misapplying it. The reason for this is simple: Regardless of one's desire or training to get the externals right, *real success in this area is largely determined by the internals*. Stated differently, it is difficult for a boss to regularly deliver criticism with care if that boss does not in fact care.

For the Christian manager, then, the challenge begins by examining one's attitude toward those who underperform or misbehave on the job. Is it primarily an attitude of impatience and frustration, or an attitude of humility and servant-like concern? Does one see the employee as a dry well or as deep water? The internal reality will ultimately govern the external practice.

As usual, we have choices here. God gives us the freedom to select our attitude toward problematic subordinates, to select our words, and to select our correctives. We may not be able to remedy all behavior and performance problems, but we can always approach the feedback process in a God-honoring manner.

NOTES

1. This anecdote compiled from the following sources: Eric Malni, "City Worker Held After 4 Supervisors Are Slain," *Los Angeles Times*, 20 July 1995, A1; Paul Feldman, "Shootings Spark Calls for Better Security Measures," *Los Angeles Times*, 21 July 1995, B1; Stephanie Simon and Paul Feldman, "Search Goes On for Answers to Violence in the Workplace," *Los Angeles Times*, 30 July 1995, B1; Patrick McGrcevy, "Suspect Kept Gun at Work, Records Show," *Los Angeles Daily News*, 10 August 1995, 4; Janet Gilmore, "Ex-City Worker Handed Life Term," *Los Angeles Daily News*, 8 February 1997, 4.
2. "Study: Evaluations Spurring Worker Aggression," *The Houston Chronicle*, 10 April 1996, 4.
3. For a detailed listing of these approximately two dozen incidents, see Stephen Goods, "Cases of Workplace Attacks This Decade," *The Hartford [Connecticut] Courant*, 7 March 1998, A7.
4. For a representative sampling of this literature, see: Daniel R. Ilgen and Carol F. Moore, "Types and Choices of Performance Feedback," *Journal of Applied Psychology*, 72, no. 3 (1987): 401–406; Kathryn Tyler, "Careful Criticism Brings Better Performance," *HR Magazine*, 42, no. 4 (April 1997): 57–61; Jeffrey A. Mello, "The Fine Art of Reprimand: Using Criticism to Enhance Commitment, Motivation and Performance," *Employee Rela-*

tions Today, 22, no. 4 (Winter 1995): 19–28.

5. More information on speaking from the "I" perspective is available in Roger Fisher and William Ury, *Getting to Yes: Negotiating an Agreement without Giving In,* 2nd ed. (New York: Viking, 1991).

REWARD EMPLOYEES WITH PRAISE

A young man walked into a diner and asked to use a pay phone. The waitress behind the counter pointed him in the right direction and then eavesdropped as the man made his call.

Once connected to his party, the young man said in an enthusiastic voice, "Hello, Mr. Anderson. My name is Patrick DeBerg and I was just calling to ask whether you'd be interested in hiring a bright, hardworking sales manager to oversee your marketing staff. . . . Oh. . . I see. . . . You already have a bright, hardworking sales manager? OK. Well, thanks anyway."

The young man walked back to the counter with a smug grin on his face, an expression that perplexed the waitress. "What are you smiling about?" she asked with a touch of attitude. "You just got turned down!"

"Well, actually," the young man replied, "I didn't. You see, *I am* that 'bright, hardworking sales manager.' I just wanted to make sure that my boss thought so too!"

This modern-day parable is, for good reason, becoming well-worn in both pulpits and business schools across the country. Pastors and professors like to remind their listeners that people want to know that others recognize their contribution. In fact, employees value such recognition more than almost anything else in the workplace. That's not to minimize the importance of things like fair pay, job security, interesting work, and advancement opportunities. But beyond these obvious motivators, people also need to hear that they are doing well and that their effort is appreciated.

This need is so strong that a lot of the time, if starved for gratification, people will fill the void by shamelessly generating self-congratulations. Consider the all-too-familiar scenarios. Doesn't almost every workplace have at least one person who has made a habit of telling people how busy he or she is? Aren't there some people at work who regularly steer conversations in the direction of what they've achieved or expect to achieve? Hasn't each one of us, at one time or another, subtly sought positive reinforcement from a superior who chose to keep it to himself? The desire for recognition is simply part of human nature.

At the same time, though, workplace accolades appear to be less available than in former days. Although the boss who makes praise part of his or her routine is not yet extinct, this person has been on the endangered species list for some time. Whether this is because managers are now more busy, or more prideful, or because they no

longer see offering compliments and encouragement as part of their job, bosses who regularly reward with praise are the exception rather than
the rule.

That's unfortunate, especially since many experts have advocated using employee praise as a
no-cost motivational tool. It's even more unfortunate when one considers that this commonsensi-
cal recommendation has been around for about
three thousand years.

PROVERBS ON PRAISING OTHERS

Proverbs has a lot to say on this topic—a testimony to the issue's significance. In particular, it
counsels us on the value of praise as well as on
the specifics of how and when to bestow it. The
proverbs contain at least five reminders on why
and how to praise our subordinates and colleagues. Let's look briefly at each.

Offer Praise as a Reward

From a divine perspective, how important is
praising others? So important that God punctu-
ates His book of wisdom with words about the
value of praise. Indeed, He concludes Proverbs
with a discourse that applauds "The Wife of Noble Character." Proverbs 31 is the capstone of the
book; its final twenty-two verses present this
woman as one to admire, a remarkable person by
any standard.

The woman celebrated as ideal in Proverbs 31
is one who hand-knits clothing and linen, who
brings food from great distances, who cares for
her family day and night, and takes care of the
poor and needy. This tireless woman also plants

vineyards and even owns a profitable business. She speaks with wisdom and has no anxiety about the future.

Given those impressive attributes, how should one thank such a woman? What does she deserve as recompense? The last two verses of Proverbs answer this very question:

Charm is deceptive and beauty is fleeting; but a woman who fears the Lord is to be praised. Give her the reward she has earned, and let her works bring her praise at the city gate.
(Proverbs 31:30–31)

Among the many things that can be said of this passage, three points stand out for our purposes here. First, we learn that praise of another individual is a reward—and not just any reward. *Praise is the consummate reward for a job well-done.* Proverbs does not say that this prolific worker should get a merit raise, a bonus, a new Lexus chariot, or a weekend at the Jerusalem spa. Instead, the ideal reward for the ideal woman is that she be *praised*.

Second, the very last verse of Proverbs tells us the central reason that we should not neglect praise: It is something one has "earned." That is, similar to a paycheck or a promotion, recognition of another's accomplishments is portrayed as a responsibility we have toward each other. The praiseworthy individual is *entitled* to our acclaim.

In our present cultural context, though, it would be easy to discount this notion of entitlement, since it seems like just another in the endless parade of contrived entitlements that people are now demanding. However, our culture should not blind us to an important truth: God does not regard praising subordinates as pandering. It is not just some politically correct alternative to genuine management. Rather, praise is an integral part of God's compensation and motivation program.

Praise in Public Whenever Possible

A third lesson from the passage is that we should praise one another "at the city gate." In ancient times, cities were like fortresses, built with huge, protective walls surrounding them. The walls were continuous except for the several city gates that were opened during daylight hours to permit people to come and go. Because of the gates' central location and proximity to visiting travelers, goods were routinely traded and legal matters were handled just inside those gates.

It is in this high traffic area that Proverbs 31:31 says that the wife of noble character is to be praised. *Recognition of one's good works, the verse says, is best done publicly.* Public veneration elevates the honor. It renders the praise even more rewarding to the individual who has earned it, since everyone now knows what this person has accomplished. Moreover, from a management perspective, public praise is also effective because it plainly signals to others what constitutes commendable behavior.

Christ used this approach as well. When He lauded Peter for confessing Jesus as Messiah, Christ did so in front of all the other apostles (see Matthew 16:17–20). When Christ praised a sinful woman for her repentance at His feet, Christ was surrounded by Pharisees (see Luke 7:44–47). And when the centurion demonstrated trust in Christ's power, Jesus turned to those following Him and said: "I tell you the truth, I have not found anyone in Israel with such great faith" (Matthew 8:10). In doing these things, Jesus not only validates praise as a reward, He also models for Christians the public behaviors we are to emulate.

Praise Should Be Timely

Notice, too, that in all of these instances, Jesus praised not just publicly, but also *immediately*. Christ did not delay but, instead, seized the moment to acknowledge a person who had earned it. Proverbs 15:23 parallels this teaching:

A man finds joy in giving an apt reply—and how good is a timely word!

Untimely praise may be empty praise. As is true of any behavior, a significant gap between the behavior and the reward undermines the re-inforcement potential of that reward. By con-trast, "timely" words are fruitful words. They are an "apt reply" to a deserving individual.

The *New Revised Standard Version* and the King James Version further illuminate this timing element by rendering the Hebrew: "a word in season, how good it is!" NRSV; ["is it" KJV]. In those translations, the proverb implies that the praise need not be instant, but it should be in reasonable proximity to the behavior. God's wisdom invites us to acknowledge praiseworthy behavior sooner rather than later—in season rather than a few seasons down the line.

Praising Others is Gratifying

Proverbs 15:23 also notes that the timely, apt reply brings joy not just to the hearer, but to the deliverer as well. Most of us have experienced the pleasant sensation of passing along deserved recognition, so the text serves not as a revelation but as a reminder that this "joy" comes to those who freely praise others. Moreover, as will be discussed in the next major section of this chapter, "joy" may come in another form to the manager who habitually praises subordinates: It may come in the form of a more loyal, more productive, more committed workforce.

Praise Can Be Nonverbal As Well

Lastly, Proverbs counsels us that the bestowal of praise need not be one-dimensional; instead, it can be communicated through various avenues. Two verses attest to the fact that something as simple as a look can have a revitalizing effect:

*A cheerful look brings joy to the heart,
and good news brings health to the bones.*
(Proverbs 15:30)

> *When a king's face brightens,*
> *it means life; his favor is like*
> *a rain cloud in spring.*
> (Proverbs 16:15)

These texts not only further support the value of praise (figuratively speaking, praise "brings joy to the heart" and "health to the bones"); they also inform us that the mere expression on a manager's face can have lasting, positive effects on subordinates. One has many options for lauding others' accomplishments, but we should not forget—especially when pressed for time—that beyond the standard verbal and written "that-a-boy," and beyond the employee-of-the-month plaque and the name in the company newsletter, simply a "cheerful look" is a reward. When the "[leader's] face brightens," Proverbs 16:15 tells us, it is akin to something that was life-giving to the community that originally received the wisdom: a spring rain cloud that would nurture crops and produce an abundant harvest.

Today, such an expression on the boss's face remains a sign of good things to come. And it costs a manager nothing! Building "life-giving" morale does not get any more inexpensive than this.

SOME INSIGHTS FROM THE ACADEMIC AND PRACTITIONER RESEARCH

Findings from academic researchers affirm scriptural teaching and provide some additional aspects to consider.[1] First, there is little debate about the biblical and intuitive notion that employee recognition can have a positive effect on one's performance.[2] It is generally agreed by both academics and practitioners that periodically acknowledging an employee's contribution is critical for both learning and motivation.

Second, most managers do not offer enough praise, in part because supervisors tend to underestimate the importance that subordinates attach to feedback and to overestimate the value of formal rewards.[3] As a result, it is often the case that informal, positive feedback is only available when employees proactively seek it out for themselves.[4] The practitioner literature affirms these conclusions as well; the staunchest proponents of narrowing the praise gap are best-selling authors Ken Blanchard and Bob Nelson.[5]

Third, positive reinforcement tends to be most useful if it actually indicates *why* the employee's performance was effective.[6] The statement: "You did a first-rate job on the report, Dan; nice work!" is certainly better than saying nothing, but it also omits crucial reinforcing information. Taking the time to explain why it was "nice work" (e.g., the report was clear, it was succinct, it was creatively formatted) increases the likelihood that the specific commendable behavior will be repeated in the future.

Fourth, in situations where both positive and negative feedback will be given (e.g., a performance review), researchers have found that subordinates are more likely to accept the negative feedback as accurate if the positive feedback is offered first.[7] The practitioner literature is quick to add, though, that whenever possible, positive and negative comments should be delivered separately. Appending a "but on the other hand . . ." to an accolade, many rightfully argue, has the effect of nullifying any beneficial aspects of praise.[8] Whenever possible, then, avoid following bad news on the heels of good.

Finally, it is not always the case that more praise is better. There is apparently a point of diminishing returns. On the academic side, one of the best field studies to date concluded that feedback every two weeks is about as effective as feedback every week.[9] From the practitioners, we hear that employees occasionally have a cynicism about excessive praise from above and infer that it may just be a tool to manipulate them into working harder.[10] Furthermore, excessive praise can culminate in employee insensitivity to that positive feedback, so to maximize its impact, praise should be used judiciously.

MAKE PRAISE STANDARD OPERATING PROCEDURE

Neglecting to give credit and thanks where it is due can affect both the commitment of the slighted individual and the supervisor's relationship with this individual. We've all been there, having earned something yet having seen it withheld for no reason other than apparent ingratitude. Whether this occurs in the workplace, in a marriage, or in some other capacity of servanthood, that withholding is at the very least frustrating. And over time, it engenders resentment, disloyalty, a "do-the-minimum" mind-set, and in some cases, a severing of the relationship. Under-appreciation will indeed have its consequences, largely because it is the delinquent remission of what has been "earned."

Accordingly, in a business context, Scripture invites every manager to make employee acclamation standard operating procedure. One CEO made this a routine by placing five coins in his pocket at the beginning of each day and then moving one coin to the other pocket each time he complimented a subordinate. In another case, a restaurant owner whose schedule was too hectic to recognize his staff during work hours took a few minutes after closing time to jot personal notes to those who made a real difference that day.[11]

There are no organizational constraints tying a manager's hand in this area, so the possibilities for making employee commendation a habit are unlimited. The challenge for the Christian manager, then, is to adopt one of these possibilities in order to more faithfully reward employees with the praise they have earned.

NOTES

1. Much of the following is derived from the literature review of Wayne F. Cascio in *Applied Psychology in Human Resource Management*, 5th ed. (Upper Saddle River, N. J.: Prentice Hall, 1998), 270–71.
2. Daniel R. Ilgen, Cynthia D. Fisher, and M. Susan Taylor, "Consequences of Individual Feedback on Behavior in Organizations," *Journal of Applied Psychology*, 64, no. 4 (1979): 349–71.
3. Martin Greller, "Evaluation of feedback sources as a function of role and organizational level," *Journal of Applied Psychology*, 65, no. 1 (1980): 24–27.
4. David M. Herold and Charles K. Parsons, "Assessing the Feedback Environment in Work Organizations: Development of the Job Feedback Survey," *Journal of Applied Psychology*, 70, no. 2 (1985): 260–305.

5. Kenneth Blanchard and Spencer Johnson, *The One Minute Manager* (New York: William Morrow, 1982); Bob Nelson, *1001 Ways to Reward Employees* (New York: Workman, 1994).

6. Jacob Jacoby et al., "When Feedback Is Ignored: The Disutility of Outcome Feedback," *Journal of Applied Psychology*, 69, no. 3 (1984): 531–45. See also Joseph J. Martocchio and James Dulebohn, "Performance Feedback Effects in Training: The Role of Perceived Accountability," *Personnel Psychology*, 47, no. 2 (1994): 358–73.

7. Dianna L. Stone, Hal G. Gueutal, and Barbara McIntosh, "The Effects of Feedback Sequence and Expertise of the Rater on Perceived Feedback Accuracy," *Personnel Psychology*, 37, no. 3 (1984): 487–506.

8. See, for example, Bob Nelson, "Try Praise: It's the One Incentive Any Small Company Can Afford," *Inc.*, 1 September 1996, 115.

9. Jagdeep S. Chhokar and Jerry A. Wallin, "A Field Study on the Effect of Feedback Frequency on Performance," *Journal of Applied Psychology*, 69, no. 3 (1984): 524–30.

10. See, for example, Mark H. McCormack, "Being Praised Isn't Always What It Seems," *The [Cleveland] Plain Dealer*, 3 June 1997, 12C.

11. Both of these examples come from Bob Nelson, "Try Praise," *Inc.*, 1 September 1996, 115.

REWARD EMPLOYEES WITH PROFITS

In 1990, Sears, Roebuck & Company adopted a new revenue-generating strategy for their auto centers. The objective was to encourage customers, whose cars were already in the shop, to purchase more preventative maintenance services. So, as standard procedure, Sears' mechanics were now to apprise customers of pending vehicle problems and solicit them to immediately address these problems.

To ensure that the mechanics would in fact do this, Sears did what many companies do when seeking to shape employee behavior—they modified their compensation system. Instead of a strict hourly pay system, mechanics' compensation would now be a combination of base pay and commissions. Hourly pay rates would be cut by about one-third and mechanics could make up the difference through their commissions on the services that they sold.

Nice idea. But unfortunately, the endorsement of piecework by the Chicago headquarters prompted local managers nationwide to add a few variations of their own to the commission system. Many managers imposed sales quotas on their mechanics for high-margin items like shocks, springs, and brakes, and for "hard-to-question areas" like front-end alignments. A mechanic's failure to meet these quotas met with stiff penalties—anything from undesirable work schedules to demotion to dismissal. Moreover, now that commissions were available, some managers refused to give any more raises in hourly pay, telling mechanics, "If you want a raise, you have to go out and sell more services."

Predictably, these new and improved compensation strategies produced perverse results. Mechanics, most of whom were having difficulty recovering their lost wages, began recommending unnecessary work and charging for work not performed. When ordering parts, they tended to purchase the most expensive ones, thereby increasing their commission. They would often neglect time-consuming tasks like wheel balancing in favor of more profitable activities and quota work. And occasionally, vehicles even incurred damage while in the shop, thus increasing the cost to fix them.[1]

But Sears' consumers suspected foul play. In California, after a three-year, 50 percent rise in complaints about Sears Auto Centers, the State Consumer Affairs Department went undercover, bringing dozens of vehicles with very modest repair needs to Sears. The department estimated that *on average*, they were overcharged by $223 per visit! Officials in New Jersey conducted a similar investigation, concluding that in *every visit* to Sears, mechanics recommended unnecessary repairs.

After the abuses were made public on both coasts (the California Consumer Affairs Director went so far as to call this "the systematic looting of the public"), forty-three other states quickly pursued their own claims against Sears. The ultimate settlement included the distribution of $20 million in Sears coupons to bilked consumers, the payment of millions of dollars to the states for their attorney fees, and the scrapping of Sears' commission and quota systems. Perhaps even more expensive for the company was the loss of both the public trust and the countless valuable mechanics who quit their jobs.[2]

Sears had adopted the age-old compensation strategy of paying workers based on their performance. That strategy is rapidly becoming the norm rather than the exception. More than two-thirds of U.S. companies now have some type of incentive system in place, ranging from merit pay and commissions to gain sharing and employee stock ownership plans; and a 1995 survey found more than 40 percent of firms have specifically designed such a program for nonexecutive employees.[3]

In principle, these variable-pay schemes are a good idea, given their potentially profound effect on individual motivation and productivity. But as the Sears case demonstrates, they are also fraught with risk. Workers tend to do what the reward system motivates them to do—both the positive and the negative—so any performance-based pay system must be designed with the utmost care and forethought.

This applies also to profit-sharing programs, one of the more alluring and controversial pay-for-performance strategies. It's not a new idea—in the United States, profit sharing traces its roots back to the late 1700s—but it's only in recent decades that it has become institutionalized in American business. Recent surveys indicate that between 18 and 20 percent of U.S. companies now have some sort of profit-sharing program in place.[4]

Interestingly, though, besides being endorsed by a wide array of CEOs, the concept of sharing profits with employees is also endorsed by Scripture.

PROVERBS ON SHARING ONE'S WEALTH

A general principle espoused in the Book of Proverbs—and indeed throughout the whole Bible—is *one honors God and is blessed when one is benevolent to those less fortunate.* Typical of these Scriptures is Proverbs 22:9:

*A generous man will himself
be blessed, for he shares
his food with the poor.*

At first glance, a verse like this seems to warrant little explication. The message appears basic and self-illuminating. But, as usual, there is more to the message of this proverb and others like it (such as Proverbs 14:21; 19:17; 28:8) than we glean from a flat reading of the text. To fully appreciate its implications, we must understand it as a manifestation of a teaching that dates back to Israel's Torah, the first five books of the Old Testament.

Showing Justice and Kindness

Among Moses' last words to Israel, he said: "Do not be hardhearted or tightfisted toward your poor brother. . . . Give generously to him and do so without a grudging heart; then because of this the Lord your God will bless you in all your work and in everything you put your hand to" (Deuteronomy 15:7,10). Indeed, this reveals a duty to share one's wealth; however, beyond obligation or sacrifice, sharing with the needy was considered an integral component of the Israelite ethic of *mishpatim:* justice and kindness toward strangers. God commands this thirty-six times in the Torah, more times than He mentions any other religious responsibility, so for Israel, justice toward one's neighbor was not simply an ideal toward which one should strive. And it was not merely a laudable societal goal. Rather, acting justly and charitably toward others was *absolutely central* to being God's faithful people. That is, *mishpatim* was part of the covenant God made with Israel: Because you are My chosen people, act in justice toward your neighbor.

Accordingly, for an individual or community to violate this instruction implied not only a breaking of the law but evidence of a deliberately created rift in their relationship with God—a repudiation of the sacred covenant. This is why, for example, the polemic of the prophet Amos was so virulent (e.g., Amos 2:6–7; 5:11–12). Israel had been systematically exploiting its needy and, in doing so, forsook its special relationship with God.

So when we read what Proverbs 22:9 says about sharing food with the poor, we should remain mindful of its historical context: To neglect the poor implied personal rejection of God; to be generous was to give Him glory. The proverb's message is not primarily about sacrifice of food, but instead it's about making a choice regarding our relationship with our Creator. Rejection or honor. There's no middle ground.

And it's a message that transcends time and Testaments. It reverberates from Moses to Solomon to the prophets and, ultimately, to Christ Himself as He delivers those familiar words: "Whatever you did for one of the least of these brothers of mine, you did for me" (Matthew 25:40). Then and now, when the elect share food with the poor, they do it for God.

Sharing the "Bread" of Business

Centuries later, in a modern business context, it is not a stretch to conceptualize the "food" of one's business—its sustenance—as the excess that allows it to survive, its profit. And rather than hoard it, distribute it exclusively to owners, or reinvest all of it, Scripture invites those responsible for such decisions to generously share the bread of business with those less fortunate than they.

The implications are many. Among them are business tithing, investing in the local community,

opening new facilities in disadvantaged neighbor-
hoods, and hiring some folks who would otherwise
be considered unemployable. Understandably,
pursuits like these are unsettling to some because
they will generate a zero or even negative financial return. But one does not give food to get
more food back.

Then there's profit sharing, the one business
application of Proverbs 22:9 where the financial
payback can be extraordinary. As such, sharing
profits with employees—and especially low-paid
(i.e., "poor") employees—resides squarely in the
intersection of meeting individual needs and responsible corporate stewardship. It is an extension of proverbial wisdom that can honor both
God and the other bottom line.

WHAT WORKS AND DOES NOT WORK IN
PROFIT SHARING?

Beyond the "justice" dimension of profit sharing, let's think about profit sharing's financial impact on an organization. Sharing profits should
both increase employee productivity and de-
crease turnover, according to widely advanced
theories.[5] Linking part of one's pay to firm performance could elicit more effort from that individual, say the theorists. And, because workers
are rewarded as a group under this program, they
may be more willing to share information and to
operate as a team. Regarding turnover, since
profit sharing tends to elevate employee compensation to a level that is above the market (an "efficiency wage" in economist-speak), employees
may be more reluctant to leave the firm. Moreover, above-market wages may also reduce shirk-

ing of duties, since the cost to the employee of being fired is not just a job search, but probably a lower wage at the end of that search.

Qualified Findings

Well, these are theories. And we have a particular reason to be skeptical here. We know from experience that such hypotheses often originate in political and social agendas rather than economic ones. Ivory-tower types and policy wonks regularly advocate profit sharing under the guise of enhancing organizational performance, but it may be little more than a transparent initiative for social reengineering. So when one sifts through the voluminous research and commentary on profit sharing, one should be cautious to separate the wheat from the chaff.

Of course, there is some wheat, or substance, in the research. Even though the empirical work has not yet conclusively demonstrated a clear, causal effect on productivity, turnover, and profits,[6] a few large-sample, well-designed studies exist that point us toward preliminary conclusions about what works and does not with profit sharing programs.[7] Moreover, their findings are bolstered by an abundance of anecdotal evidence.

On the downside, these studies show that profit sharing can degenerate into nothing more than an added cost of operations. The research confirms that *where employees do not perceive a direct linkage between their effort and the size of their profit-sharing check, their effort and decisions to stay with the organization will be unaffected by any profit-sharing plan.* Moreover, even if there is a perceived linkage, a small profit-sharing bonus has little impact on individual outcomes. Similarly, a deferred bonus (e.g., profits put into the employee's pension account rather than offered as cash), no matter the size, has no discernible effect on current productivity.

That may seem like common sense. Behaviors are highly correlated with valuable and immediate rewards whether we're training a dog, raising a toddler, or managing employees. However, the simplicity of this principle appears to escape those designing many of the profit-sharing plans. According to a 1997 study, 42 percent of companies still base rewards on criteria that employees cannot directly influence (e.g., stock prices, earnings per share).[8]

Effective Profit-Sharing Programs

Notwithstanding the pitfalls, though, profit-sharing programs can work and have worked. Here are a few factors that the empirical studies have identified as influencing their success. *First, company size appears to be an important variable* in the equation. Smaller companies (775 employees or fewer) tend to experience productivity increases of between 11 and 17 percent, whereas in larger firms, the effects range from 0 to 7 percent. Seemingly, a larger workforce makes the individual behavior-bonus linkage more tenuous and can create more of a "free rider" problem.

Second, profit sharing tends to be especially useful where costs of monitoring employees are high. As is true of any effective pay-for-performance system, when employees perceive that real and meaningful rewards will flow from augmented effort, they will require less supervision of their diligence. The research has correlated profit-sharing with dramatic reductions of supervisory costs.

Third, the best empirical work has demonstrated that *profit sharing can lead to lower turnover,* especially where profit sharing substitutes for part of base pay, rather than being gravy on top of base pay. The precise cause of this is still a matter of debate, but from a statistical perspective, the relationship is undeniable.

And as to the ultimate question in the board-room—does profit sharing increase profits?—the jury in the research community still remains out. But a plethora of anecdotal evidence suggests significant effects on corporate financial performance. Here is but one testimony to profit sharing's impressive potential to both resuscitate and reinforce a business.

A Case Study: Cin-Made

In the introduction we met Robert Frey; remember his plight? He had purchased Cin-Made, a small manufacturing company that was replete with labor problems: astronomical labor costs, contentious union-management relations, an embarrassing 75 percent on-time shipping rate, and a dismal and volatile bottom line. As we noted then, Frey had several options, according to prevailing management theory. Here's what he did.

To remedy some of Cin-Made's financial woes, Frey purchased faster machinery and sought wage concessions of 25 percent. His three dozen workers, whose jobs had not changed in decades, outright rejected the new technology, ostensibly because they feared injury with faster equipment.

And as far as wage concessions, the knee-jerk response was a prolonged strike. Eventually, they came back to work at a 12.5 percent pay cut, but Frey's "victory" here only won him "a factory full of angry, defeated employees determined to oppose any innovation and grieve every tiny infraction of the letter of the contract," Frey admitted.[9]

Through these cost-reduction initiatives, Cin-Made's profits stabilized a bit. But Frey knew that he had yet to identify a long-run solution for the company. So he tried something radical. He proposed giving employees 30 percent of pretax profits and keeping the books open for the union scrutiny. He held monthly state-of-the-business meetings with employees to let them know how the company was doing. And he gave them more managerial responsibilities (e.g., problem-solving, cost cutting, allocating overtime, interviewing applicants) to give them a personal feel for management's concerns.

In essence, his strategy was to sensitize workers to the financial and marketing realities of the business and to give them a stake in the outcomes. He sought to achieve that elusive objective of aligning worker and employer interests.

The first four years of this new approach met with lackluster results. Thirty percent of small profits translated into small bonuses and little change in the work culture. Since 1989, though, Cin-Made's profit has been strong and, consequently, annual profit-sharing checks have represented on average a 36 percent increase in pay. In a factory of a few dozen employees, the linkage between individual effort and bonus size was readily apparent, and as Frey's employees began realizing the fruits of their labors, their commitment and contribution increased commensurately.

Today, Cin-Made boasts a 98 percent on-time delivery record, a productivity level up 30 percent from the mid-1980s, very low absenteeism, and a workforce that meticulously monitors waste and temporary employees. Strict adherence to job descriptions is a thing of the past, grievances are down to one to two *per year*, and labor relations are peaceable. Tri-annual wage negotiations proceed from the premise that any increase in fixed wages or benefits comes out of profit sharing, so the negotiations tend to be amiable. According to Frey, this chunk of money belongs entirely to the employees, so they can have it in whatever form they want it.[10]

Like at Lincoln Electric (see Principle 9), employees choose to perpetuate and depend on the pay-for-performance system. Their mind-set has been transformed. They think like managers, they consider themselves to be on the same side of the table as their CEO, and they work collectively to enlarge the pie for everyone involved.

A WIN-WIN SOLUTION

It would intolerably strain the scriptural text to say that there is any *mandate* in Proverbs for profit sharing. However, profit sharing does seem to be a legitimate extension of the prudent teaching that we honor God by sharing our resources with those who have little. That would seem particularly the case for the lowest-level employees.

Moreover, but in our context secondarily, it can also be an effective business tool, since, if implemented properly, sharing profits can align the interests of employees with those of the employer and the company's owners. It therefore represents a scripturally sound, win-win solution. Profit sharing is a reward strategy that both satisfies employee economic needs and encourages them to care more about customer service, cost containment, and quality.

NOTES

1. "Sears Abuses Detailed, Workers Laud Crackdown on Auto Shops," *Los Angeles Daily News*, 12 June 1992, B1.
2. "Sears Gives Coupons to the Clipped," *Newsday*, 30 October 1992, 53.
3. The 1995 survey of 1,383 companies by Towers-Perrin Co. is summarized by Jay Matthews, "Pay Raises Give Way to Bonuses," *The Washington Post*, 21 July 1995, B3. The 1997 Hewitt Associates study found more than two-thirds of companies surveyed (189 firms) used an incentive system, as reported in Julie Johnsson, "Bonus Bust: Firms Fumble Cash Payout," *Crain's Chicago Business*, 1 December 1997, 1.
4. Martha Priddy Patterson, "Retirement Benefits in 1995: KPMG's Third Annual Survey Findings," *Journal of Compensation and Benefits*, 1, no. 3 (November/December 1995): 15–22. See also the 1995 Towers-Perrin survey as summarized in *Employee Benefit Plan Review*, "Nontraditional Pay Practices on the Rise," 50, no. 4, (October 1995): 51.
5. For some of the better theoretical work on this subject, see Martin L. Weitzman and Douglas L. Kruse, "Profit Sharing and Productivity," in Alan S. Binder, ed., *Paying for Productivity* (Washington D. C.: The Brookings Institution, 1990); and Douglas L. Kruse, "Profit Sharing and Productivity: Microeconomic Evidence from the United States," *The Economic Journal*, 102, no. 1 (January 1992): 24–36.
6. The most comprehensive empirical treatment of this topic to date is Douglas L. Kruse, *Profit Sharing: Does It Make a Difference?* (Kalamazoo, Mich.: W.E. Upjohn In-

stitute, 1993).

7. In addition to Kruse's 1992 and 1993 studies (see notes 5 and 6), other work used for this section includes Sushil Wadhwani and Martin Wall, "The Effects of Profit Sharing on Employment, Wages, Stock Returns and Productivity: Evidence from UK Microdata," *The Economic Journal*, 100, no. 3 (March 1990): 1–17; and Felix R. FitzRoy and K. Kraft, "Cooperation, Productivity, and Profit Sharing," *Quarterly Journal of Economics*, 102, no. 1, (1987): 23–35.

8. Julie Johnsson, "Bonus Bust: Firms Fumble Cash Payout," *Crain's Chicago Business*, 1 December 1997, 1.

9. Robert Frey, "The Empowered and the Glory: A Firm's Turbulent Turnaround," *The Washington Post*, 26 December 1993, H1.

10. Frey, "The Empowered and the Glory," *The Washington Post*, 26 December 1993, H1; and "CEO Finds Empowerment Pays," *The Cincinnati Enquirer*, 29 July 1993, B9.

PART FIVE

CONTROLLING WORKPLACE CONFLICT

RESTRAIN WORKPLACE GOSSIP

Cyber-gossip is the newest innovation in an ancient practice. Notwithstanding this new-and-improved medium for gossip, E-mail, the destructive effects remain the same. One now-former employee of a firm bears personal witness to this.

Linda says her stomach still churns when she thinks back to her early days on E-mail. One fateful workday, rather than gossiping in quarters where she could be overheard, Linda took advantage of the then-novel computer technology to send a quick message to a peer in her department. The note was essentially a lambasting of a supervisor named Mark, affectionately referred to in the message as "Marky-poo," among other things.

When completed, Linda cheerfully and covertly sent her critique. Problem was, as a relatively inexperienced user, she sent the message not to her colleague, but to Mark himself! Ouch.[1]

Gossip can be defined as discrediting talk

about someone who is not present. And if it pervaded the workplace before, the widespread use of E-mail for exchanging information—its use as a "virtual watercooler"—has only served to exacerbate the practice. Rumors, innuendo, and other juicy tidbits can crisscross the office and the world today at E-speed, often leaving no one the wiser. One can even seem to be working diligently at a terminal when, in reality, one is merely working the rumor mill.

Of course, the "meet me at the photocopier" approach has not become obsolete—and it likely never will since people can't seem to help but talk about others. Typical of the survey results on the prevalence of gossip is the finding by the American Society for Training and Development that 21 percent of people say they are "frequent participants" in workplace gossip, and 64 percent say they gossip at work "sometimes." The research concluded that gossip is often work-related, usually centering on business changes, office intrigue, and people's private lives.[2]

If the statistics were not disheartening enough, there's also the glowing assessment of gossip by the "experts." Scholars from the fields of psychology, sociology, anthropology, and even philosophy tell us that workplace gossip is beneficial because of its ability to "bond" individuals together. According to one psychology professor at Temple University: "If people aren't talking about other people, it's a signal that something is wrong—that we feel socially alienated or indifferent."[3]

The academics' seeming commendation of gossip is seconded by the news media. Newspapers and magazines regularly portray gossip as having a gainful dimension to it. Consider the following headlines:

- "Pssst: Office Gossip Can Be a Productive Tool" (*Indianapolis Business Journal*)
- "Listen Up! Gossip Can Be Good; Gossip, Experts Say, Is Simply an Act of Spreading Information" (*Fort Lauderdale Sun-Sentinel*)
- "Profit from Gossip" (*The Times of London*)
- "In Praise of Office Gossip" (*Fortune*)[4]

In spite of these pronouncements, the truth remains: Workplace gossip fuels conflict, disruption, underperformance, and turnover. And what makes the secular commentary even more baneful is that it couldn't be more antithetical to the scriptural teaching on this subject. Both the Old and New Testaments clearly reject secular notions about gossip, and the counsel to eschew gossip appears most prominently in the Book of Proverbs.

PROVERBS ON GOSSIP

In our contemporary setting, one could surely ask in good faith: "What's the big deal here? Everybody gossips and usually there's no malicious intent behind the words. We in business should just lighten up and focus on matters of genuine consequence."

A legitimate contention, perhaps? Try telling that to the apostle Paul, who set the sin of gossip alongside some pretty extreme company. To the Romans, he wrote about some in their community: "They have become filled with every kind of wickedness, evil, greed and depravity. They are full of envy, murder, strife, deceit and malice. They are gossips, slanderers, God-haters, insolent, arrogant and boastful" (Romans 1:29–30). And to the Corinthians, he similarly wrote: "I fear that [when I see you] there may be quarreling, jealousy, outbursts of anger, factions, slander, gossip, arrogance and disorder" (2 Corinthians 12:20b). The inclusion of gossip in such lists may appear to be grievously misplaced in a present-day culture that renders gossip at worst a tepid sin. But God views it differently. It is not by accident that His inspired messenger to the Gentiles numbered gossip with these flagrant transgressions. Gossip is a venomous misuse of the tongue, induced by its scriptural companions arrogance, jealousy, insolence, and the like. Gossip is a manifestation of those negative attitudes and a vehicle by which our underlying problems create strife.

Whereas this linkage to strife may be only implied by Paul, it is made explicit in Proverbs:

Without wood a fire goes out;
without gossip a quarrel dies down.
(Proverbs 26:20)

Strife feeds on gossip as fire feeds on wood, according to the proverb. *A remedy for conflict, then, is to starve the fire by minimizing gossip*. Among the many possibilities to execute this teaching,

Proverbs highlights one in particular: Do not associate with gossips. Proverbs 20:19 teaches that:

A gossip betrays a confidence;
so avoid a man who talks too much.

We find very little ambiguity or wiggle room here. The verse tells us not to encumber ourselves with people who gossip. We are to deliberately "avoid" them. And in extreme cases, it would seem, we are called to remove them from our organizations.

The apostle John lends further support to this somewhat controversial position. In his third epistle, he wrote to praise a man named Gaius who provided hospitality and support for brothers in the faith. In doing so, John took the occasion to also alert the community about the problematic tolerance of their church boss, Diotrephes. Apparently, Diotrephes, a man "who loves to be first" (note the connection to arrogance), had been "gossiping maliciously" about John and had furthermore been kicking good people out of the church (3 John 9–10). In the letter, John promised to personally remedy the situation when he arrived. Here, arrogance led to gossip, which led to a strife that was impairing effective witness and growth. To break the chain, John indicated, Diotrephes the gossip must be silenced or jettisoned.

Applying all of this to a contemporary business setting, the Scriptures teach not only that gossiping is a sin and that unchecked gossip creates conflict, but also that *it is entirely appropriate to restrain workplace gossip through policy*. It is to the implementation of this thorny issue that we now turn.

CRAFTING A REASONABLE POLICY

Several business management journals have in recent years urged employers to regulate workplace gossip.[5] However, any time one promulgates rules that constrain employees from engaging in what they might consider to be natural or innocuous behaviors, one must do so with two eyes focused squarely on the reasonableness index. Such a task cannot be undertaken in a cavalier manner, since overregulation can be as fruitless as no regulation at all.

Case in point: the no-gossip policy for employees of the City of Baton Rouge. Here a policy regulating the speech of city employees blossomed to prohibit the telling of *any joke* that could possibly be construed by someone as sexist or racist. That is, any joke that gave offense to any person could bring the offending employee up for censure or worse. Later, the city council recognized that, although the latter part of the policy was well-intended, there were inherent problems with proscribing joke telling.[6]

The trick, then, is to craft a no-gossip policy that honors God without unduly suffocating employee interaction. It must meet organizational interests of extinguishing rumor and encouraging respect, while simultaneously treating adults as adults. One way to perform this balancing act is by (1) narrowly tailoring the policy to deal only with gossip and (2) focusing the policy more on education about the problem than on punishment. The former prevents the policy from evolving into the untenable (as in Baton Rouge), while the latter maximizes the chance that it will be effective.

The educational dimension, it seems, is especially important because the average person in the workplace has never really thought about gossip being detrimental to morale, teamwork, or productivity. Quite the opposite, people tend to view it as a normal and even healthy activity that somehow makes them feel good. Therefore, to get any employee to buy in to the policy, one must encourage employees to see what management sees—that gossip leads to strife, and strife undermines the quality of the work environment. Whatever the vehicle one chooses for announcing one's no-gossip policy (office memo, formal brochure, agenda item in a meeting, etc.), education about this rationale should be the centerpiece of the communiqué.

One might then consider following up this initial education about gossip by again raising to the surface (during, say, performance reviews, mentoring sessions, or training) the negative effects of disparaging talk about others. As with any new policy, "continuing education" about the policy's purpose and its parameters will be necessary for it to gain a real foothold in a work group. Additionally, a manager can facilitate such education by providing information about how an employee can personally extinguish workplace gossip when it arises. Both Christian resources and the empirical literature offer useful tips on how to diplomatically steer conversations away from gossip.[7]

Of course, the no-gossip policy cannot be *exclusively* educational since a law without teeth is no law at all. There must be some established consequence for violation of the policy. Common sense should be one's guide here; penalties must fit the crime, and, most importantly, a manager should remain mindful of the principles of due process described in the next chapter. However, remembering the warning in Proverbs 20:19 "to avoid a [gossip]," management should be sure that the policy underscores that severe and repeated violations of the no-gossip policy are cause for dismissal.

As the policy matures though, self-enforcement may prevail in lieu of the more severe tactics. That is, by raising consciousness about this issue, by focusing on education about the effects of workplace gossip, and by offering regular reminders that management is indeed serious about this issue, one can gently shape a workplace culture so a stigma is associated with gossiping. Just as it has become socially unacceptable to use vile language or to dress suggestively in some workplaces, it can become similarly unacceptable to make derogatory remarks about others. Herein lies the long-term ideal for any no-gossip policy. If narrowly tailored and educationally oriented, after years of its operation it may become institutionalized as part of the corporate culture.

TREATING THE SYMPTOMS ONLY

When people are exposed to one another for prolonged periods of time, there is a vast potential for some to develop a distaste for others in the group. And often this distaste will manifest itself as gossip. It is important to recognize, therefore, that a no-gossip policy will treat only symptoms of broader problems like disrespect, envy, vengeance, and arrogance. It will not (nor should it attempt to) change people's attitudes toward one another. Personnel policy is insufficient for this larger task.

What the policy can do for an organization, though, is to help starve the fire of conflict by depriving it of some wood. And it's not that radical or novel a concept. Hallmark, for instance, includes gossip as one of the "inappropriate uses" in its E-mail policy[8] and American Express has a hot line in place to drain gossip about workplace policies. To reduce the effect of corporate rumors and gossip, American Express employees are encouraged to anonymously call at any time to get reliable answers to their questions.[9]

There is, however, one irony in promoting a no-gossip policy for which the Christian manager should be prepared: The policy's *initial* effect may be to *increase* gossip. That is, this unorthodox approach to employee management may simply give workers one more thing to gossip about and, even more disturbingly, the manager whose name is on the memo may be the target of choice for some time to come!

But this is part of the price paid by Christians when we advance Bible-based ideas that perplex the world. Scripture tells us that the workplace grapevine—like every gossip medium—is often a poison grapevine. Therefore, though others may question or criticize us, we should remember when we administer an antidote that it is another way we honor God and those He has placed under our care.

NOTES

1. Vicki Vaughan, "E-mail's Burning Up the Electronic Grapevine," *Austin-American Statesman*, 21 November 1993, E1.
2. "Did You Hear It Through the Grapevine?" *Training and Development*, 48, no.10 (1 October 1994): 20.
3. Robin Westen, "The Real Slant on Gossip," *Psychology Today*, 17 July 1996, 44–48.
4. Reported in *Indianapolis Business Journal*, 20 November 1995, 37; *Fort-Lauderdale Sun Sentinel*, 1 May 1994, 1E; *The Times of London*, 12 August 1996, 13; and *Fortune*, 19 August 1985, 253–56, respectively.
5. See, for example, Elizabeth Danzinger, "Minimize Office Gossip," *Personnel Journal*, 67, no. 11 (November 1988): 31–34; William C. Bruce, "Employers Have Reputations to Uphold," *Business Insurance*, 6 July 1998, 31–33; and John Chanin, "Draft a Clear Policy on Office Romance," *Denver Business Journal*, 19 September 1997, 28A.
6. Shanna Labourdette, "Measure Institutes New Policy Manual," *The Baton Rouge Advocate*, 17 May 1995, 5B.
7. See, for example, Michael A. Zigarelli, *Christianity 9 to 5: Living Your Faith at Work,* (Kansas City: Beacon Hill, 1998), 30–33, which draws on findings and citations from Donna Eder and Janet L. Enke, "The Structures of Gossip," *American Sociological Review*, 56, no. 4 (August 1991): 494–508.
8. Jenny C. McCune, "Get the Message: Email Is Great, but It Can Be Too Public, Too Casual and Too Dangerous," *Management Review*, 86, no. 1 (1 January 1997): 10–11.
9. Anna Jones, "Psst . . . Gossip Can Start a Walkout," *The Independent–London*, 3 April 1997, 13.

ENSURE DUE PROCESS

After gaining national recognition for his work in the field of politics, professor Harmon Zeigler was recruited away from the University of Oregon to teach at the University of Puget Sound. Because his classroom performance matched his research acumen, students lined up to take his courses, notwithstanding his reputation for being a tough grader. One autumn day in 1992, though, Zeigler suddenly found that he had another reputation as well—this one quite undeserved.

The letter from the dean came out of nowhere. In disbelief, Zeigler read that three unnamed students had accused him of sexually harassing them and that the university had found the charges to be credible. Accordingly, because Zeigler "pose[d] a threat of immediate harm to the university community," he was being given the choice to resign or be terminated.

Zeigler was instantly in the dean's office to sort out the problem. Clearly there must be some mistake, Zeigler argued, because the allegations simply were not true. Furthermore, he wanted to know who was accusing him and what type of investigation the university could have possibly conducted without ever questioning the accused.

But the renowned scholar was stonewalled by his boss. The decision had been made. These women "were absolutely determined to proceed with legal action," said the dean to Zeigler, so "we've got to get you out of here."[1]

Although the women never sued the university, Professor Zeigler did, seeking damages for a litany of torts including wrongful discharge. A predominantly female jury decided the case in Pierce County Superior Court after hearing from students, faculty, administrators, and even psychiatrists. They heard sordid tales that Zeigler claimed had no basis in fact, and they heard lengthy testimony about the university's dubious investigative procedures. The record indicated that in the mere three days between accusations and forced resignation, the university had done almost nothing to substantiate the accusers' claims. It did not follow its own sexual harassment code, it gave Zeigler no chance to defend himself, and it treated Zeigler far more harshly than other faculty members who had *admitted* propositioning female students. Regardless of whether Zeigler ever did anything improprietous, the jury concluded, the investigation was devoid of procedural due process and that was simply unfair. One and one-half million dollars unfair, said the jury, who found the school negligent in causing emotional distress to the professor.[2]

Similar stories have surfaced coast to coast, with jurors almost always siding with the plaintiff. Another professor who was forced out on the heels of spurious charges won $805,000 from the University of Maine.[3] A Houston police officer who was falsely accused of running his hands up and down the legs of a female clerk gratefully accepted a check for $3 million from the city after his day in court.[4] And a terminated Phillip Morris sales rep similarly won a $1.2 million judgment after an Illinois court concluded that the company had conducted "an incomplete investigation of the truth of the [accusations]."[5] From a legal liability perspective, ensuring due process in the workplace—whether an employee is charged with sexual harassment or some other violation of company policy—appears more important than ever.

This is true from a managerial perspective as well, since the fair and timely resolution of conflicts can streamline a work system, reduce disruption, help to retain good people, and ultimately save money. And although grievance systems are historically identified with unionized firms, today almost half of the largest nonunion corporations have a formal procedure in place for addressing employment disputes.[6] It's just smart business.

It's "wise" business as well. Beyond these legal and managerial concerns lies a biblical perspective: Proverbs alerts us to the pitfalls of ignoring due process and calls for justice in the workplace.

PROVERBS ON DUE PROCESS

Due Process in Early Israel

For the people of Old Testament Israel, due process for all was steeped in the tradition of the Torah. Due process was considered neither a luxury nor an option; rather, it went to the heart of Israel's covenant with the Lord. In particular, three passages from the law illustrate both the roots and the rigidity of this instruction:

> *Do not deny justice to your poor people in their lawsuits. Have nothing to do with a false charge and do not put an innocent or honest person to death, for I will not acquit the guilty.* (Exodus 23:6–7)
>
> *Do not pervert justice; do not show partiality to the poor or favoritism to the great, but judge your neighbor fairly.* (Leviticus 19:15)
>
> *And I charged your judges at that time: Hear the disputes between your brothers and judge fairly, whether the case is between brother Israelites or between one of them and an alien. Do not show partiality in judging; hear both small and great alike.* (Deuteronomy 1:16–17a)

There are no limiting or qualifying phrases here, nor have there been throughout time. Due process is an elemental principle of human interaction. In fact, the principle even transcended the millennia to reside prominently in no less a document than the United States Constitution. With echoes of Israel's sacred law, the Fifth and Fourteenth Amendments state that no person shall be deprived of "life, liberty, or property, without due process of law."

Substantive and Procedural Due Process

Not surprisingly, then, the Book of Proverbs also picks up on these divine mandates, speaking to both "substantive" and "procedural" due process concerns. *Substantive due process* refers to the content, or substance, of a particular law, policy, or remedial action. According to Black's Law Dictionary, sixth edition, it is the requirement that a law "be reasonable in content as well as in application" and its goal is "protection from arbitrary or unreasonable action." In an employee-management context, it would mean that personnel policies are fair to all parties involved and applied in a way that the innocent are deemed innocent and the guilty deemed guilty.

Procedural due process is a component of this. It refers to the manner in which decisions are made, and is defined simply as "the guarantee of procedural fairness."[7] In employee management, this would entail that any conflict resolution system include sufficient procedural safeguards so that both accuser and accused are treated fairly throughout.

Two proverbs powerfully communicate these concepts. The first is Proverbs 17:15:

Acquitting the guilty and condemning the innocent— the Lord detests them both.

The verse is a call to ensure substantive due process. The guilty should not go free nor should the innocent be convicted. And it's surely no trivial matter. This is one of those relatively rare instances where the Bible says that God "detests" something. As discussed when covering dishonesty in Principle 6, such language is designed to be both exceptional and arresting. It intends to capture our attention when we may be immersed in a sea of other Scriptures. "Listen very carefully," the proverb tells us. "Stop at this point in the lesson and pay closer attention: God *detests* injustice, so eradicate it where you can."

Part of that eradication involves the use of proper procedures when evaluating any given situation. That is, for substantive due process to exist, procedural due process must be safeguarded. Proverbs 18:17 identifies one of those safeguards:

The first to present his case
seems right, till another comes
forward and questions him.

When we hear one person's account of something that has happened, the natural inclination is to consider that account credible. When a friend or colleague tells us about some injustice that he or she has endured, our tendency is to agree with them that things are amiss. Similarly, when we hear a trial lawyer present a closing argument, the argument appears quite compelling—"till another comes forward."

There's always at least one other side to any story. Proverbs 18:17 reminds us in almost humorous fashion that there is folly in our commonplace practice of trusting the first account to which we are exposed. It pokes fun at our naive embrace of a one-sided tale and in the same breath calls us to correct this procedural short-coming.

Cross-examination, this verse says, is essential to due process, as is the opportunity to defend oneself. Without such basic procedural safe-guards, substantive justice is compromised. This may seem obvious, but managers charged to re-solve conflicts sometimes forget it—or deliberately ignore it. Why? Sometimes an overworked, under-funded manager, burdened with time or budgetary constraints, may rush to a premature judgment. Other times, fear of a potential public relations disaster may spur management to quickly douse the growing fire. As we saw in the anecdote that opened this chapter, though, circumventing due process can be an expensive blunder. And as we see in Scripture, there are no adequate "business reality" excuses for sidestepping these manageri-al responsibilities.

Overall, then, Proverbs directs us to be exceed-ingly fair in resolving conflicts. It echoes God's age-old attitude toward injustice and under-scores the importance of sound investigative practice. In the workplace, the Christian manag-er is to take heed of what God detests and, when probing disputes, ensure fairness to all parties in both procedure and substance.

THE CURRENT PRACTICE OF DUE PROCESS

The Move Toward Mediation of Disputes

Many organizations have found that due pro-cess for employees, aside from being ethical, can operate to the advantage of its own bottom line as well. In fact, furnishing due process through alternative dispute resolution (known as ADR) is currently one of the hottest topics in employee management precisely because of its win-win nature. Formal complaint resolution can preserve relationships and save employers money, while simultaneously furnishing due process to employees who may have had little before. A recent Cornell University study of 528 Fortune 1000 firms reveals the extent of ADR's popularity, with the most noteworthy results being:

- 88 percent of firms used mediation in the past three years
- 79 percent of firms used arbitration in the past three years
- The most widespread business use of mediation and arbitration is in commercial and employment disputes
- 54 percent said that cost pressures affected their decision to use ADR[8]

These are promising findings. The implementation question, though, can be a bit vexing. How can an organization eliminate strife and maintain relationships—the goal of a formal complaint review—while at the same time containing costs?

A Case Study

One answer comes from a Texas-based company called Brown & Root.[9] In 1993, this large engineering and construction firm was sued by an employee for sexual harassment. Ultimately, the company won the case, but the victory still significantly disrupted their work environment and cost them $450,000 in legal fees. Moreover, the battle had permanently altered the careers of several employees, including the plaintiff. The experience led Brown & Root to pursue a better way to resolve workplace conflict—a way that would meet the interests of both employer and employee.

Soliciting input from approximately three hundred employees, Brown & Root devised a system by which all employment disputes would be addressed internally, and where any employee with a grievance could get a fair, expeditious resolution to the problem. The four-option program gave grievants the choice of: (1) using the firm's open-door policy to speak with one's immediate supervisor or a higher level manager, (2) conferring with a company dispute resolution representative who investigates the problem and proposes a settlement, (3) requesting formal mediation through an outside mediator, or (4) resolving the issue through final and binding arbitration. The catch for employees, however, was that to be employed at Brown & Root one had to waive one's right to sue over employment disputes—a quid pro quo whose legitimacy has been sanctioned by courts all across the country.[10]

From an employee standpoint, this trade-off might be a fatal flaw in the "new-and-improved" conflict resolution system. Few individuals want to abdicate their rights to a judicial forum. But through its early solicitation of employee input, the company was alerted to this potential flaw. Accordingly, says William Bedman, Brown & Root's associate general counsel, the company came to recognize that the long-term success of the program would depend not just on management commitment, but also on its equitable and uniform application.[11] *The solution, therefore, was to safeguard due process.*

And they have in many ways. First off, the system is accessible to every employee. Options one and two cost the employee nothing, and for options three and four, the employee pays only $50 for the mediator or arbitrator and the company picks up the rest of the tab. The employee always has a right to hire an attorney of his or her own choosing and, since many might have trouble affording this "right," the company again provides a subsidy. Brown & Root will reimburse 90 percent of the employee's legal fees up to an annual cap of $2,500.

Secondly, the system appears to be fair both procedurally and substantively. The rules of the American Arbitration Association (AAA) guide mediations and arbitrations. Both the mediators and arbitrators are selected jointly from a list of AAA neutrals. There are adequate opportunities for discovery (the pre-hearing process of seeking evidence from the other side). And tellingly, the size of the settlements has been similar to the days when Brown & Root employees took their employer to court.

Importantly for both sides, justice comes swiftly as well. During the first five years of its operation, the program handled about 3,000 grievances of every kind, ranging from wrongful discharge and harassment to scheduling conflicts and leave requests. Forty percent of these were resolved within a month of filing, and 75 percent were resolved within eight weeks. Only 40 of the 3,000 cases went to arbitration which, although it is a longer process, is still significantly shorter than litigation.[12]

And what of the effects? By the company's estimates, legal expenses from employment disputes are now down between 30 and 50 percent from the pre-program costs, and overall the annualized price of the program is substantially less than what one large court settlement would cost both sides.[13] Moreover, by tracking complaint patterns so carefully, the company can correct systemic or recurring problems before they blossom. Turnover is down as well. Brown & Root claims that since its inception the dispute resolution program has helped retain more than three hundred valuable employees.

Operational fairness is the secret to this program's success. It is what has made Brown & Root a household name in dispute resolution circles. Building on a sensitivity to due process, the company has designed an effective system of conflict management that works to the advantage of all stakeholders.

DEVELOPING A FAIR AND COST-EFFECTIVE SYSTEM

A legitimate system of workplace due process entails several things. Among the most basic elements are accessibility for all employees, prior notice that certain behaviors are unacceptable, prompt and thorough investigation when those behaviors allegedly occur, a chance for all concerned parties to tell their side, an impartial judge or group of judges, and consistent treatment in enforcement. The system should reliably find the innocent to be innocent and the guilty to be guilty, and punishments must fit the crimes.

However, the system need not be formal or expensive for it to be fair. Especially in smaller operations, simple open-door policies can often secure workplace justice as effectively as elaborate peer review boards, arbitrations, or mediations—if, that is, the policy is administered scrupulously. One way to determine a policy's effectiveness is this: Does the person charged with resolving the dispute care enough about procedural and substantive due process to protect the rights of everyone involved? A positive answer indicates a fair, properly enacted policy.

And when that decision maker is a Christian, the answer must be an unequivocal "yes."

Christians—and Christian managers—worship a just God, so others should see this justice through us. We worship a God who is concerned about acquitting the innocent and convicting the guilty; as Christian managers we should be equally concerned. Accordingly, each time a dispute arises among one's subordinates, and each time a subordinate is accused of some sort of misconduct, the Christian manager is presented with an opportunity to model God's nature by ensuring due process in resolving the matter.

NOTES

1. Ruth Shalit, "Sexual Healing: The Accused Get Even," *The New Republic*, 27 October 1997, 17.
2. Steve Maynard, "Ousted UPS Prof Wins $1.5 Million Judgment," *The [Tacoma] News Tribune*, 2 July 1994, A1.
3. John Ripley, "Dinsmore Awarded $805,000; Jury Agrees Former UMFK Professor Was Wrongfully Fired in '92," *Bangor [Maine] Daily News*, 11 March 1995, 1.

4. Ruth Shalit, "Sexual Healing: The Accused Get Even," *The New Republic,* 27 October 1997, 17.

5. *Gibson v. Philip Morris, Inc.,* 685 N.E.2d 638, 645 (1997).

6. U. S. Dept. of Labor, Office of the Secretary, *Fact-finding Report Issued by the Commission on the Future of Worker-Management Relations,* 2 June 1994 (Washington, D.C.: Government Printing Office), 254.

7. *Black's Law Dictionary,* 6th ed., s.v. "procedural due process" (St. Paul, Minn.: West Publishing, 1990).

8. David B. Lipsky and Ronald L. Seeber, "The Use of ADR in U.S. Corporations," report from Cornell University, School of Industrial and Labor Relations, Ithaca, N. Y. (1997). An executive summary of this report can be found on the Worldwide Web (www) at www.ilr.cornell.edu/depts/icr/new/execsum.html.

9. Information on Brown & Root comes from the following sources: Michael A. Verespej, "Sidestepping Court Costs," *Industry Week,* 247, no. 3 (2 February 1998): 68–71; Sally Roberts, "ADR Helps Contain Costs," *Business Insurance,* 10 March 1997, 3–4; Carol Wittenburg, "And Justice for All," *HR Magazine,* 1 September 1997, 131–33; Dominic Bencivenga, "Fair Play in the ADR Arena," *HR Magazine,* 1 January 1996, 50–52, and from the Brown & Root website (www.halliburton.com/bus.asp).

10. For more information, see Michael A. Zigarelli, "Compulsory Arbitration of Non-union Employment Disputes," *Human Resource Management Review,* 6, no. 3 (1996): 183–206.

11. See William L. Bedman, "From Litigation to ADR: Brown & Root's Experience," *Dispute Resolution Journal,* 50, no. 4 (1995): 8–15.

12. Michael A. Verespej, "Sidestepping Court Costs," *Industry Week,* 247, no. 3 (2 February 1998): 68.

13. Wayne N. Outten, "Negotiating and Drafting Severance Agreements on Behalf of Employees," a report of the Practicing Law Institute, Washington, D.C., October 1996,1001, n. 5.

DISCHARGE
THE
DROSS

The hotel chain Days Inns of America began as a Christian-based company. Its founder, Lon L. Day Jr., sought to honor God by running family-oriented facilities, by not serving alcohol, by giving away more than 2.5 million Bibles to customers, and by offering a large share of the profits to charity. For his fifteen-year effort, Day prospered, growing the company to more than three hundred locations.

Day also cared immensely about his employees and even hired four full-time roving chaplains to assist workers who were in need. At the same time, workplace incidents, such as taking kickbacks and harassing female coworkers occasionally dictated that problematic employees be terminated. According to Day, dismissed employees would typically plead their case with a fervent: "You can't fire me. I thought this was a Christian company!"

Day's response to them was simple. "God will always give you a second chance, but you have had your second chance with us!"[1]

Some managers have no difficulty letting employees go, but for others, the prospects of terminating a subordinate can turn the most seasoned business professional into a nail-biting novice. And when that professional is also a Christian, there's the added difficulty of reconciling the firing with God's call to servanthood, forgiveness, and love. As a result, exiting people from the organization against their will is perhaps the most arduous of employee-management tasks for the Christian manager.

However, one thing must be made clear in any book on Bible-based management: *Nowhere does Scripture support the notion that it is sinful or even a poor witness for an overtly-Christian boss to fire a subordinate.* God's Word does not per se prohibit firing people. Quite the opposite, as we'll see momentarily, under certain circumstances terminating employees is both sanctioned and encouraged in Scripture.

But it is also the case—and this cannot be overemphasized either—that beyond the due process concerns discussed in Principle 18, and beyond the ubiquitous governmental restrictions in this area, there are myriad other responsibilities that God's law imposes on Christians before we can invoke the workplace version of capital punishment. As usual God has set a higher standard of conduct for those who follow His Son and, again as usual, some of the clearest teachings on this subject derive from Proverbs.

PROVERBS ON
TERMINATING EMPLOYEES

Should the Manager Forgive?

As we've noted, most Christian businesspeople are perplexed, even confused, by the question of termination. On one hand, we know that grace is the central pillar of the New Covenant. The Cross is God's sacrifice for the forgiveness of our sins, and as God forgives us, so too should we forgive others (Ephesians 4:32). Firing is not forgiveness. In fact, it appears to be the radical opposite! Moreover, even in the Old Testament, as illustrated by Proverbs 19:11, we read of the virtues of forgiveness and patience with those who have offended us.

---

*A man's wisdom gives him patience;
it is to his glory to overlook an offense.*

So we Christians are undoubtedly to model God's grace for those who work for us. That's uncontroverted. The problem is that both Testaments also unmistakably state that it is wholly appropriate to excommunicate individuals from a group because of their behavior.

Grace versus Discipline

The tension seems to be the grace to overlook an offense versus the necessary discipline for violating rules. In Proverbs, two passages stand out in this regard:

*Drive out the mocker, and out goes
strife; quarrels and insults are ended.*
(Proverbs 22:10)

*Remove the dross from the silver,
and out comes the material for the
silversmith; remove the wicked
from the king's presence, and his
throne will be established
through righteousness.*
(Proverbs 25:4–5)

Proverbs 22:10 makes plain that the removal of problematic individuals has the effect of reducing conflict. Digging a little deeper, the word translated here as *mocker* carries the connotation of *scorner* and *arrogant talker*. This is a person whose inflated sense of himself creates disputes and generally disrupts the work environment. The verse gives us the green light to oust such people from our workplaces.

Proverbs 25:4–5 builds on this thought with a promise that goes beyond limiting conflict. *Dross* is the residue left behind after an ore has been purified by fire. From the smelter emerges the pure element, in this case, silver, that is productive material for the smith. Likewise, for a work group to be as productive as possible, its dross, that is, its "wicked"—those disloyal in words or deeds to the leader—and by implication its "mockers," must be driven out. What should be the natural result of this "purification" process?

The proverb teaches that the king's "throne will be established through righteousness"; in a modern business context, the purging of these employees from the group paves the way for effective, God-honoring leadership.

We find a parallel and familiar New Testament instruction in 1 Corinthians 5, where Paul upbraided the community for tolerating an unrepentant, sexually immoral church member. The individual should be immediately expelled, the apostle wrote, because of his potential contamination of the membership. "Don't you know that a little yeast works through the whole batch of dough?" Paul asked them rhetorically. He instantly offered the remedy: "Get rid of the old yeast that you may be a new batch" (1 Corinthians 5:6–7).

The Scriptures from Proverbs and 1 Corinthians suggest a tension in the text between forgiveness and expulsion—a tension that lies at the heart of the Christian manager's confusion about discharge. Since competing actions are described by God, what is God's will in this area?

THREE BIBLICAL LESSONS
ABOUT POSSIBLE TERMINATION

As is often the case in Scripture, it is through wrestling with seemingly incompatible texts that we ultimately recognize God's instructions. By harmonizing passages that point in different directions, we often gain comprehension of a more intricate scriptural principle not articulated in any one passage. Through these texts, God actually offers three lessons for the Christian manager who is contemplating an employee's discharge.

First, the tension in these teachings can be interpreted as a divine reminder that there is seldom a quick and easy answer to serious, potentially job-ending offenses. In business, we sometimes treat such problems as having a simple solution, but this is faulty judgment. God shows us through His dual teaching that the Christian manager should never impetuously fire a subordinate, nor should he or she naively overlook every offense. Neither extreme satisfies the biblical edict. Lesson one, therefore, is *avoid hasty decisions about firing or retaining employees*, opting instead for the more time-consuming path of circumspection and prudent reflection.

Second, the Bible instructs that the prevailing attitude throughout the decision-making process must be one of patience and forgiveness. Of the two teachings that hang in tension with one another, grace is clearly the superior one. This again does not imply that one can never fire an employee. That's an oversimplification. Rather, lesson two is that, for the decision maker, *grace must envelop law at every stage of this uncomfortable process*. In practice, this would mean that the Christian manager should offer employees opportunities to correct problems, should evaluate whether employee difficulties are really a function of poor management, and should consider assisting employees who face dismissal from the organization. (Further implications of this lesson are presented in the next section.)

Lesson three is that *occasionally it will be not only appropriate but actually advisable to drop an employee from the payroll.* From a scriptural perspective, an individual who hampers one's leadership, who arrogantly scorns others, who perpetually creates conflict, who is corrupt, or who cannot follow the work rules is tantamount to "dross" that must be removed for the common good. The Christian manager, like all other managers, has a duty not just to employees, but to all other stakeholders as well. Responsible corporate stewardship will sometimes dictate that troublemakers, criminals, and even underperformers have their relationship with the organization involuntarily severed. There is no sin in this if it is done with the proper attitude and using the proper procedures.

Overall, then, harmonizing the difficulties in Scripture gives way to important insights on a complex issue. God calls the Christian manager to always invest significant time and energy in this consequential decision, judiciously balancing compassion and standards—grace and law— whenever the question of termination arises.

TERMINATION TIPS BASED ON SCRIPTURAL AND SECULAR REALITIES

Legal and Safety Considerations

Even those who do not recognize God's prescription to terminate with care often do so anyway. That's largely because employee dismissal has evolved into risky business in the United States. First off, there's the $64,000 question on every manager's mind: "Will we get sued?" (Actually, the question tends to be worth significantly more than $64,000 these days.) Governmental scrutiny of the employment relationship is everywhere, from federal, state, and local statutes to administrative regulations to common law. One can hardly establish policy or make any employee-management decision without considering Big Brother's opinion. Moreover, Equal Employment Opportunity Commission statistics attest that there is even more cause for concern than in years past. Employee discrimination charges rose more than 25 percent during a recent six-year period, from about 64,000 in 1991 to over 80,000 in 1997.[2]

Beyond insulating themselves from legal liability in termination, managers must also consider the safety factor. According to the Bureau of Labor Statistics, assaults are the second leading cause of workplace fatalities (behind transportation accidents),[3] and many of these are triggered by post-termination anger. Stories of disgruntled ex-employees stalking their former boss or barging into the human resources department with a baseball bat have become commonplace in past decades, prompting managers to pay increased attention to termination protocol.

Lastly, there's the revenge of the nonlitigious, nonviolent individual. People who are angry about their discharge are finding increasingly creative ways of getting revenge on their old boss, from divulging corporate secrets, to sabotaging computer files, to creative financial paybacks. For example, several years ago, a Chicago restaurant called the Party Tavern and Grille closed down without any notice to employees. To make matters worse, the employees' final paychecks bounced while the owners continued to operate another restaurant across town. One laid-off employee evened the score by taking his family to his ex-employer's other restaurant, ordering about $600 worth of food and wine, and then presenting the bounced check in lieu of payment![4]

The point is, reasons abound to hone one's termination skills. Consequently, useful practitioner literature now exists to fine-tune these skills. Borrowing from this literature, what follows here are some termination tips that do not contravene God's standards.[5]

Understanding Employment Law

Most experts in employee dismissals recommend that the manager have a general familiarity with the structure and parameters of employment law. Given the pervasiveness of the law, that is wise counsel. The basic structure of the law is that an employer has a free hand to discharge for any reason *unless the employer is constrained by some law, some court case, or some contractual arrangement*. That is, the default condition, called "employment-at-will," does not require an employer to have a performance-related reason or any just cause to dismiss an employee. The only requirement is that the job action not be motivated by criteria prohibited in antidiscrimination laws, judge-made common law, or contract.

Space limitations preclude a fuller explication of the legal requirements, but several resources exist both in book form and on the Internet to furnish the manager with a more complete overview of the legal dimension of employee management.[6] As a primer, though, Table 5 presents a snapshot of the current legal boundaries.

Table 5

A BASIC OVERVIEW OF EMPLOYMENT LAW

LAW	BASIC PROVISION	ENFORCEMENT AGENCY
Title VII of the Civil Rights Act of 1964	Prohibits discrimination on the basis of race, color, religion, national origin, and sex	Equal Employment Opportunity Commission
Age Discrimination in Employment Act	Prohibits discrimination against individuals age forty and over	Equal Employment Opportunity Commission
Americans with Disabilities Act	Prohibits discrimination against any individual who meets the definition of "disabled" and requires reasonable accommodation of disabled employees and applicants	Equal Employment Opportunity Commission
National Labor Relations Act	Prohibits discrimination on the basis of one's union status or support	National Labor Relations Board
State and local statutes	These laws parallel the provisions of federal laws to cover employers of every size (federal law typically applies to employers of fifteen or more employees). Some states and cities also extend antidiscrimination law by prohibiting employer actions based on marital status, sexual preference, smoking habits, and other criteria.	State human rights agency or State Department of Labor City administrative agencies for city ordinances

Law	Basic Provision	Enforcement Agency
Common law	Most states, through judge-made law, prohibit employer actions that would undermine public policy (e.g., terminating employees for serving jury duty) or that violate the employer's own personnel handbook. A handful of states have even gone further in common law to require that the employer keep all of its promises, whether written or verbal.	No enforcement agency; employee plaintiffs must retain their own legal counsel and pursue their claims in state court

Stemming in large part from the legal concerns, the practitioner literature also urges complete consistency in how and why employees are dismissed. Dischargeable offenses should remain dischargeable offenses across time, and due process procedures should not vary with the nature of the wrongdoing. If one employee gets an internal hearing, all employees should have this right. If an employee is given a last chance after failing a drug test, similarly situated employees should be extended that courtesy. In general, the more consistent one's dismissal procedures are across terminations, the less ammunition an employee has to claim discriminatory or wrongful discharge.

Next, and again deriving from the legal concerns, a manager should document everything— from performance deficiencies to behavior problems to conversations with the employee. Moreover, incidents and other problems should not be documented without the employee's knowledge. When a manager makes it a practice to caution or counsel the employee with each successive problem, termination will seldom come as a surprise. And fewer surprises translate into fewer aggressive or costly employee responses.

Lastly, and somewhat counter to the conventional wisdom, it is a good practice to *dismiss early in the week rather than later*. Traditionally, employees have been let go on Fridays. But anecdotal evidence suggests that this simply prompts the employee to stew all weekend and react more violently on Monday. Dismissing early in the week undercuts the festering effect because the employee can begin seeking employment the very next day.

Conducting the Termination Meeting

All of the points in Principle 14, "Deliver Criticism With Care," apply here; but we can underscore and add some items that are specific to termination.

First, it's always a good idea to have the meeting in a private setting. Commentators are unanimous on this point and for good reason. Public or quasi-public dismissal is humiliating and engenders revenge.

Second, keep the meeting relatively short and to the point. Criticisms should be honest and factual, avoiding subjective or insupportable conclusions. The manager should calmly explain his or her rationale for the decision and should avoid arguing with the employee. Some may find this difficult to do, especially if the employee throws the blame back to management or becomes verbally abusive. But arguing will only escalate an already tense situation, so managers should permit the employee to vent frustration without responding in kind.

Third, many recommend that a manager offer the employee a chance to resign rather than be fired. For some workers, this will seem like no choice at all, but for many others, this is an opportunity to save face. Especially for the employee who could see this coming, one may be less bitter about the situation if one can tell others that he or she voluntarily resigned. Counterbalancing this, though, it should be noted that in some states voluntary resignation will lead to the forfeiture of unemployment benefits. (Check with your state department of labor for details.)

Fourth, be sure to have all information on benefits available for the employee. Can health insurance be continued? Will there be severance pay? Will you agree not to challenge any unemployment claims if they are filed? Whatever benefits are available to discharged employees, the termination meeting is the ideal time to present them, since they offer a ray of light in an otherwise black conversation.

Looking Out for the Employee's Welfare

As discussed at various points throughout this book, there are often alternatives to firing an individual. An attitude of grace, patience, and compassion will in many cases lead to the conclusion that something more can be done to retain the individual, either in his or her present capacity or in another position. However, in those instances where one has concluded in faith that an employee should be discharged, there are a few additional considerations consistent with Scripture that the manager may want to keep in mind.

A central objective here is to avoid marring the cause of Christ in this seemingly harsh action. One way to do this is by providing enough severance pay to permit the employee to transition to another job in a financial seamless manner. Additionally, in light of God's concern for family stability, a manager may also want to take into account the individual's family situation in both the decision to terminate and the size of the severance.

Another means to keep this individual on his or her feet is either to personally provide outplacement services or to pay for a professional outplacement firm to assist the employee in locating suitable work. Drafting a letter of recommendation is similarly helpful here. If the employee is being let go simply because of a bad fit that is without remedy, provide him or her a letter for prospective employers that explains the situation.

PATIENCE, FORGIVENESS. . .
OR TERMINATION?

During the course of one's career, few managers will be able to avoid dealing with negative behaviors that must be quashed and with individuals who must be held accountable for their actions. And much of the time, the scenarios will be like nothing one could have anticipated or planned for. To cite just one example, consider the fiasco at the Bank of Boston in 1994. One fateful evening, approximately fifteen executives and sales representatives engaged in a wild, after-work party that included both male and female employees drinking "belly-shots." The object of the game was to slurp tequila from a colleague's navel as quickly as possible. When the media caught wind of this intriguing, white-collar fraternity bash, the bank had a public relations disaster on its hands.[7] If the manager responsible for disciplining these individuals is a Christian, is it appropriate to chop some heads?

As the ultimate arbiter of right and wrong, God's Word is always our guide. However, on the issue of terminating employees, Scripture does not speak so much to what constitutes "just cause" (it certainly doesn't mention "belly-shots") as it does to the manager's mind-set. As believers in the One who died for our forgiveness, grace must be the default attitude. This is what strikingly distinguishes workplace Christians from everyone else. When an employee fails in some regard (whether it be in the behavior or performance realm), *patience* and *forgiveness* should be our bywords.

They remain our bywords until some relatively nondescript line is crossed. Although Scripture is shorter on details than we might like it to be, God's Word does say that there is a point where termination is both a legitimate and invited course of action. So long as justice is administered from within an attitude of grace, disruptive or unproductive individuals can indeed be dismissed.

However, because we are dealing with people's

livelihoods here, the Christian manager must take the utmost precaution to proceed slowly and thoughtfully. *In that process, almost every principle covered in this book will apply.* Is our conclusion motivated entirely by profit concerns? Have we considered the individual's family situation? Was improper training to blame? Are we somehow breaching a trust covenant with this action? Have we really measured performance validly? Are we delivering the criticisms sensitively? Has due process been ensured? Overall, are we honoring God as Boss through our decision?

Taking God seriously has far-reaching implications for the Christian in business. It requires more effort than we'd have to expend otherwise. It demands the recognition of constraints that our peers blithely ignore. And it compels a respect for the dignity of our people that runs against the grain of most corporate cultures and perhaps against our very natures.

All of these responsibilities converge on the unsettling decision to terminate someone's employment. This may seem inconvenient and it may be time-consuming, but the willingness to faithfully obey God's mandates is the hallmark of a witness traveling wisdom's path. God does not ask that we retain every employee entrusted to us, but He always calls us to defer to His counsel and to honor His name in the process.

NOTES

1. Roger Ricklefs, "Christian-based Firms Find Following Principles Pays," *The Wall Street Journal*, 8 December 1989, 1.
2. For more information, see the Equal Employment Op-

portunity Commission web site on the Internet, at www.eeoc.gov.

3. Dean Scott, "Safety and Health: No Increase Found in Fatal Work Injuries," *Daily Labor Report,* 13 August 1998, D-11.

4. Karen Cheney, "Sticky Situations: Ready, Aim . . . ," *Restaurants and Institutions,* 103, no. 18 (1 August 1993): 125.

5. Among the sources used for this section are: Shari Caudron, "How to Terminate Potentially Violent Employees—and Live," *Workforce,* 77, no. 8 (August 1998): 44–52; Paul F. Mickey, "Tips for Handling Terminations," *Nation's Business,* 1 September 1994, 58; and Fred S. Steingold, *The Employer's Legal Handbook* (Berkeley, Calif.: Nolo, 1994).

6. See, for example, Steingold, *The Employer's Legal Handbook,* and Michael A. Zigarelli, *Can They Do That? A Guide to Your Rights on the Job* (New York: Lexington, 1994). One of the better Internet sites for both content and employment law links is the World Wide Web Virtual Library: Labor and Employment Law (University of Indiana School of Law), www.law.indiana.edu/law/v-lib/labor.html.

7. Joan Vennochi, "Bellygate," *The Boston Globe,* 1 July 1994, 65; and Kimberly Blanton, "Bank of Boston Checking Into After-Work Party by Employees," *The Boston Globe,* 6 July 1994, 30.

A STRATEGY
FOR
CONTINUOUS
IMPROVEMENT

August 10, 1978. A clear, pleasant summer's day. Three teenage girls—two sisters and their cousin—are traveling in a Ford Pinto on U.S. Highway 33 near Goshen, Indiana. The girls pull the car over to the side of the road. Minutes later, despite a dry road and visibility that is unobstructed for miles, a van plows squarely into the back of their small car. The Pinto explodes, instantly killing two girls and causing injuries to the third that will later prove fatal.

This wasn't the first time a Pinto had burst into flames after being struck from behind. Since its introduction in 1970, the Ford Motor Company had received periodic reports of similar incidents. Ford, however, did not need to investigate the cause of any of these. The company knew this was likely before it ever sold a single Pinto.

In response to the overwhelming success of the Volkswagen Beetle, and facing the specter of

the Japanese making their own incursion on the
American market, Ford had to enter the lucrative
subcompact car business fast. So, in the late
1960s, it devised a plan to produce a vehicle in
record time—twenty-five months from inception
to production (the industry average was about
forty-three months). Beyond the time constraints, top management had imposed weight
and cost restrictions on the engineering of the
car, signified in the slogan "the limits of 2,000."
The car could not weigh an ounce more than
2,000 pounds and could not cost a cent more
than 2,000 dollars.

The ambitious time and cost parameters culminated in novel production challenges. First, although an auto manufacturer usually completes
the design, styling, product planning, and engineering of a car before any production tooling is
done, for the Pinto, the tooling had to be done simultaneously with the product development.
This had the effect of "freezing" the initial basic
design of the car. That design called for the fuel
tank to be situated between the rear bumper and
axle, a mere seven inches from the back of the
car. As Ford later learned, this was a fundamental
design flaw. When Ford crash-tested several Pintos, it found that in relatively low-speed rear-end
collisions (31 mph), the rear axle studs would
rupture the fuel tank. In fact, of the eleven Pintos
crash-tested, eight suffered potentially disastrous
fuel tank punctures.[1] In tandem with sparks from
the electrical wiring in that section of the vehicle,
there was a reasonable likelihood that the car
could explode on impact.

This led to the next production challenge:

Remedying the problem within "the limits of 2,000." One option was to redesign and relocate the tank to a safer position. Ford's earlier model Capri had incorporated such a design, but time and cost precluded this approach for the Pinto. Moreover, the relocation would have reduced trunk space, something Ford considered essential to competitive sales. Another option was to leave the tank where it was, but to slightly modify it so that it would not puncture as easily. Total modification costs would be eleven dollars per vehicle.[2]

Ford did some calculations to ascertain the cost-effectiveness of the engineers' proposal. Those calculations, released in court in 1977, amounted to a cost-benefit analysis. Ford's cost to fix the problem would be eleven dollars per car times 12.5 million cars—about $137 million. It would also delay production, increase the price of the car, and marginally add to its weight. On the other side of the equation, if the company chose to do nothing, it predicted 180 deaths and 180 nonfatal burn injuries from fuel tank explosions. The forecasted court settlement by Ford was $200,000 per human life and $67,000 per burn injury. After adding in the replacement cost of the destroyed cars, Ford's projected payout if it left the design unaltered was $49,530,000.

Based on this purely financial analysis, Ford opted against making the eleven dollar safety modification to the Pinto.[3]

It is paradoxical that we live in a world that both condemns and encourages this type of thinking. The public was appalled at Ford's decision to knowingly trade off people's lives for eleven dollars per car—so appalled that Pinto has become a classic case of unethical decision making. The verdicts in the Pinto cases partially reflected this. For Ford, these were mixed. Tried in Indiana for product liability under the then-novel cause of "criminal negligence," Ford was acquitted (but later agreed to pay a nominal $22,500 to the Goshen families). In another more traditional legal case, a California jury found for a Pinto victim to the tune of $128 million. Overall, though, this example has come to represent business at its worst.

But we need not single out one organization in explaining such decision making. In almost *any* organizational setting, there are daily, sometimes incessant, pressures for managers to permit bottom-line concerns to dominate all else. In a business, that "bottom line" is of course its profit margin. In many not-for-profit organizations, it may be either "the cause" or, more basically, continued funding. In a church it might be the size of both the membership and the coffers. Worldly pressures and definitions of success subtlely and at times almost unconsciously move people toward misguided priorities, the extreme end of which is illustrated by the Pinto decision.

Since Christians are hardly immune from this workplace-induced transformation, the critical faith issue becomes: *How can the believer guard against it?* What can the Christian manager do to avoid the erosion of Christian character when immersed in an environment of secularized thinking which often minimizes ethical considerations?

The answer is hardly uncomplicated. Its many

facets are the topic of countless books that help-fully focus on a maturing, personal relationship with Christ, on a well-developed prayer life, on participation in growth groups, and so on. The Book of Proverbs also weighs in on this question, advising us that *we can guard against reliance on the world's wisdom by studying God's wisdom regularly*.

Throughout Proverbs, God urges us to make exposure to and compliance with His wisdom central in our lives. Consider two of the many passages on this point:

My son, pay attention to what I say;
listen closely to my words. Do not
let them out of your sight, keep
them within your heart.
(Proverbs 4:20–21)

My son, pay attention to my wisdom,
listen well to my words of insight,
that you may maintain discretion
and your lips may preserve knowledge.
(Proverbs 5:1–2)

Be attentive. Listen closely and well. "Do not let [these words] out of your sight. Keep them within your heart." Why? So that we can maintain discretion and speak knowledgeably—so that we will be able to consistently apply God's wisdom in a world that so often operates by a different set of rules.

These are impassioned words of a father, Solomon, to his son. And they are the God-inspired words from a heavenly Father to His children. There is an urgency in their tone. In these verses we receive some of the most important insights in all of Proverbs—insights about how to stay on course and avoid backsliding into a more secular approach to human relations. In no uncertain terms, Proverbs tells us that the consistent *employment* of God's wisdom requires the consistent *engagement* of God's wisdom.

However, it seems that relatively few Christians use Proverbs this way (or use it at all, for that matter). Too many other things occupy our time, and when we do finally get around to Scripture, too many other seemingly more important books demand our attention. Rather than relying on Proverbs to counteract the corruption of our minds, many of us only open this neglected book when we mistakenly turn there on our way to Psalms!

For those of us who, for whatever reason, overlook the Father's instruction to "pay attention to my wisdom," Proverbs 19:27 speaks bluntly to the possible consequences:

Stop listening to instruction, my son, and you will stray from the words of knowledge.

The verse tells us what we know to be true from personal experience. When there is a hiatus in our exposure to God's wisdom—when we "stop listening to instruction"—we become increasingly deaf to Scripture's advice for decision making. We tend to "stray from the words of knowledge," from God's path, in favor of the displeasing alternative. In the workplace, many of us construct our managerial house on the quicksand of human experience rather than building it on the rock of divine wisdom. The natural result is that we sink into whatever thinking pattern is typical for our organization, thereby becoming largely indistinguishable from our unbelieving and nominally believing colleagues. Sadly, our deafness to God's wisdom renders our witness mute.

As is typical of Proverbs, God sets before us two and only two paths—the paths of wisdom and folly—and encourages us to choose the more difficult one, the one that honors Him. We can invest time in God's wisdom and habitually listen to instruction, or we can go at it our own way and risk drifting.

In His grace, God has furnished us with a corrective to drifting into secularized business thinking. He has prescribed an antidote to the worldly pressures that prod us to focus on the wrong bottom line. That antidote involves scheduling time to study and to reflect on God's wisdom—to take one chapter of Proverbs a day for thirty-one days and to repeat the procedure every two or three months. Perhaps more, if possible.

Carving out five or ten minutes a day to read the proverbs powerfully combats our tendency to "stray from the words of knowledge." It can inoculate us from relying on secular thinking at work by regularly reminding us to respect and to rely on God. And if one can make time to do it in the lion's den of the workplace, all the better. God's pithy wisdom has a way of instantly crowding out whatever was motivating us moments before. It brings our work back into eternal perspective and assists us in making decisions that give Him glory.

This is God's divinely ordained strategy for our continuous improvement, to make a habit of listening to instruction. It is a strategy whose profound outcomes can be summarized no better than from Proverbs itself:

My son, if you accept my words
and store up my commands within
you, turning your ear to wisdom and
applying your heart to understanding,
and if you call out for insight and
cry aloud for understanding,
and if you look for it as for silver
and search for it as hidden treasure,
then you will understand the fear of
the Lord and find the knowledge of God.
(Proverbs 2:1–5)

NOTES

1. Dennis A. Gioia, "Pinto Fires and Personal Ethics," *Journal of Business Ethics*, 11, no. 5–6 (May 1992): 380.
2. Ibid.
3. This anecdote compiled from the following sources: Gioia, "Pinto Fires and Personal Ethics," *Journal of Business Ethics*, 379–90; and Malcolm E. Wheeler, "Product Liability: Civil or Criminal—The Pinto Litigation," *The Forum*, 17 (Fall, 1981): 250–59.